TIM FLANNERY

EXPLORING THE INCREDIBLE WORLD BENEATH THE WAVES

WEIRD, WILD, AMAZING!

ART BY
SAM CALDWELL

WATER

• FOR COLEBY AND DANIEL •

Text copyright © 2019 by Tim Flannery
Illustrations copyright © 2019 by Sam Caldwell
Design copyright © 2019 by Hardie Grant Egmont

First published in Australia in 2019 by Hardie Grant Egmont as
part of EXPLORE YOUR WORLD: Weird, Wild, Amazing!
Previously published in the US in 2020 as part of WEIRD, WILD, AMAZING!:
Exploring the Incredible World of Animals.

For information about permission to reproduce selections from this book, write to
Permissions, W. W. Norton & Company, Inc., 500 Fifth Avenue, New York, NY 10110

For information about special discounts for bulk purchases, please contact
W. W. Norton Special Sales at specialsales@wwnorton.com or 800-233-4830

Manufacturing by TransContinental

ISBN 978-1-324-01947-3 (pbk.)

W. W. Norton & Company, Inc., 500 Fifth Avenue, New York, N.Y. 10110
www.wwnorton.com

W. W. Norton & Company Ltd., 15 Carlisle Street, London W1D 3BS

0 9 8 7 6 5 4 3 2 1

TIM FLANNERY

EXPLORING THE INCREDIBLE WORLD BENEATH THE WAVES

WEIRD, WILD, AMAZING!

ART BY
SAM CALDWELL

WATER

Norton Young Readers

An Imprint of W. W. Norton & Company
Independent Publishers Since 1923

INTRODUCTION

I've been interested in animals and fossils for as long as I can remember. I grew up in the suburbs of Melbourne, Victoria, Australia, and there weren't a lot of opportunities near my home to see cool creatures. But when I was eight years old, I was walking on a sandbank at low tide and saw a strange rock. It had markings on it, and I suspected it was something special. I took it to the museum, where a man in a white coat brought me to a hall filled with gray steel cabinets. The man opened one, pulled out a drawer, and lifted out a rock identical to mine. "It's *Lovenia forbesi*," he told me, "the fossilized remains of an extinct sea urchin. They are quite common in the rocks near my home." It was, he thought, about 10 million years old. I was awestruck. Then he asked, "Are you interested in dinosaurs?"

could hardly speak. Learning about fossils led to a big breakthrough for me, and in the months and years that followed I would snorkel and scuba-dive in the bay near where I found that first fossilized sea urchin. I remember one winter afternoon, I spied a length of fossil whale jaw, nearly as long as me, lying on the bottom. Another day, I chanced upon the tooth of a megalodon shark lying in the shallows.

The man put the fossilized sea urchin back, closed the drawer, and opened another. "Hold out your hand," he said, as he placed an odd pointed rock on it. "This is the Cape Paterson Claw. It's a claw from the foot of a dinosaur, and it is the only dinosaur bone ever found in Victoria."

I held the Cape Paterson Claw! I was so excited that I

As I grew up, I went further and further afield, into the Australian desert and Great Barrier Reef, where I encountered water-holding frogs, red kangaroos, and magnificent coral. I became a mammologist—someone who

studies living mammals. For 20 years I was the curator of mammals at the Australian Museum in Sydney. I visited most of the islands between eastern Indonesia and Fiji, discovering new species of marsupials, rats, and bats. By the time I left the job I'd been on 26 expeditions into the islands north of Australia and discovered more than 30 new living mammal species.

I WAS MORE THAN INTERESTED. I WAS OBSESSED.

If you're interested in animals and nature, you can volunteer at a museum or on a dig, participate in a citizen science program like the Great Backyard Bird Count, or just start your own studies in a local tide pool or pond. If you decide to do a study by yourself, you need to take

careful notes and send them to an expert in a museum or university to check them.

If you don't live near a beach, you can study nature in a local park or backyard. The soil and plants will be filled with living things, including birds and insects. But be sure to stay safe as you investigate!

If you're interested in fossils, keep your eyes on the

rocks. Look out for curious shapes. And if you do find something, photograph it, or if it is small and portable, take it to your local museum. Most have services to help identify it.

When I was very young I often wished that I had a fun book that would tell me about the weirdest creatures on Earth. That's what I've tried to create here, for you. I hope that you find reading it to be a great adventure in itself, and that it leaves you wanting to see more of the wonderful and mysterious world around us.

Tim Flannery

CONCEPTS

EVOLUTION

Evolution is a word that describes how animals and plants change over generations. Each generation of living things is made up of individuals that differ a little from each other: some might be bigger, or more brightly colored, for example. And in nature, more animals are born (or germinate, if they're plants) than the environment can support. This means that the individuals that do best in their environment are most likely to survive. For example, if bigger, brighter animals or plants survive better, with each new generation the population will be made up of bigger, brighter individuals. Over many generations, the changes brought about by this "natural selection" can be so great that new species are created.

CLIMATE CHANGE

Earth's climate is changing because of pollution that humans are putting into the atmosphere. Greenhouse gases like carbon dioxide from burning coal, gas, and oil are causing the ground, oceans, and atmosphere to warm up. This might sound good if you live in a cold place, but many consequences of the warming are bad for living things. For example, warmer conditions mean that less water is available in some places, and creatures living in the warming oceans often have less food and oxygen. As seas rise and rainfall changes, and the atmosphere warms, entire habitats are disappearing, causing species to become threatened or even extinct.

SO SAD.

HABITATS

Habitats include places on land, in water, and even in the air. They are the places where animals live, and they vary greatly all across the world. Deserts are very dry habitats, tundras are very cold ones, while rainforests are very stable ones (with little temperature change, for example, between winter and summer). As animals and plants evolve, they become better adapted to their particular habitat. In the *Weird, Wild, Amazing!* books, habitats are grouped into four very broad categories: water, sky, forest, and desert/grasslands. Within each there are many different habitats—far too many to list.

FOSSILS

Fossils are the remains of plants and animals that lived in the past. The chances of you, or any living thing, becoming a fossil is very small. Maybe one in a billion! The first step toward a fossil being created happens when the remains of a plant or animal are buried in sediment like sand or mud. If the conditions are right, over thousands of years the sediment turns to rock, and the remains become "petrified" (which means turned to rock) or preserved in some other form, like an impression (such as a footprint).

COMMON NAMES ⓥ. SCIENTIFIC NAMES

EXTINCTION

Animals and plants have two kinds of names: a common name and a scientific name. The common name of a species is the name that you generally know them by, and these names can vary in different areas. For example, "wolf" is a common name in English, but wolves are called "lobo" in Spanish, and have many different names in other languages. But the scientific name never varies. This means that by using the scientific name, an English-speaking scientist and a Spanish-speaking scientist can understand each other.

Scientific names have two parts. For wolves, the scientific name is *Canis lupus*. The first part (*Canis*, in this case) is known as the genus name, and it is shared with close relatives. For example, the golden jackal's scientific name—*Canis aureus*—also begins with *Canis*. But the combination of genus and species name is unique. For wolves, the species name (*lupus*) means "wolf" in Latin.

Scientists use terms like "vulnerable," "threatened," and "endangered" to describe how likely an organism is to become extinct. Extinction occurs when the last individual of a species dies. If an animal is endangered, it means that very few individuals exist, and that they might soon become extinct. If an animal is threatened, it means that they are likely to become endangered in the future, while an animal being classed as vulnerable means that they are likely to become threatened.

ANIMAL TYPES

Animals and plants are classified according to their evolution. Animals, for example, can be divided into those with backbones (vertebrates) and those without (invertebrates). You can't always tell which group a plant or animal belongs to by just looking at them. Sometimes looks can be misleading! Falcons are related not to eagles or kites, which they resemble, but parrots. Parrots and falcons are classified in a group called "Austroaves," meaning "southern birds," because they originated in the southern hemisphere.

CONSERVATION

Conservation means taking care of nature and all of its plants and animals. Governments help by creating national parks, and fining litterbugs and polluters. Scientists play an important role in conservation by studying how we can help various species. You can be a conservationist in your own backyard: just plant a native tree that will become a home to the birds.

CONSERVE TO PRESERVE!

WATER

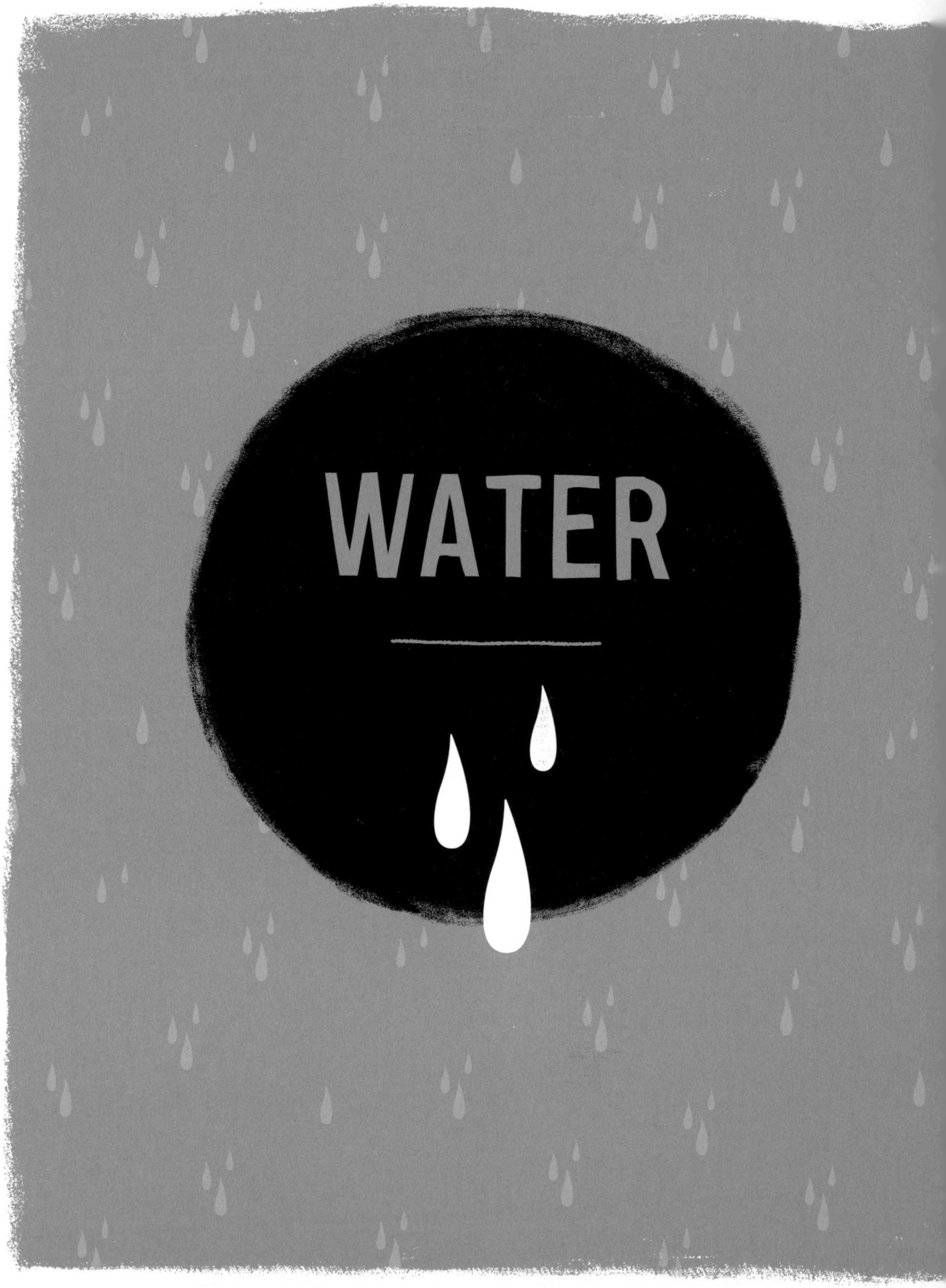

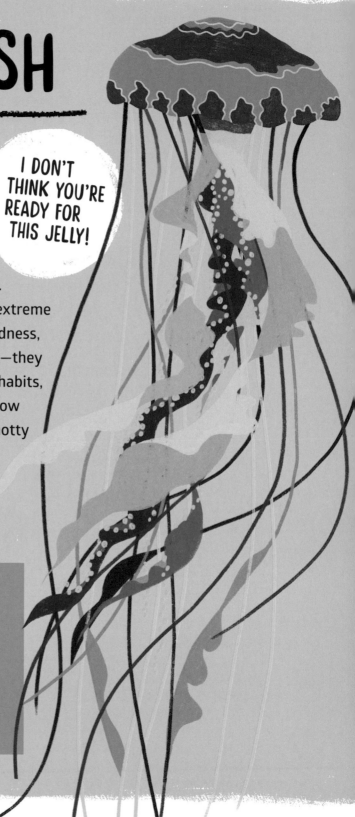

JELLYFISH

You might have come across a jellyfish washed up on the beach, or if you're really lucky you might've seen one floating gracefully along in the water. They're a fascinating mix of extreme beauty and super-slimy weirdness, and that's just how they look—they have some seriously bizarre habits, too. If you're curious about how something gets the name "snotty jelly," or whether zombie jellyfish could possibly be real, buckle up—you're about to find out.

I DON'T THINK YOU'RE READY FOR THIS JELLY!

WHERE CAN I SEE A JELLYFISH?

It doesn't matter where you live in the world—if there's an ocean near you, chances are there are jellies in it.

THE PERFECT NAME

Although jellyfish have the word "fish" in their name, they're actually not fish at all. They're related to things like sea anemones and coral. You can call them "jellyfish" or just plain "jellies."

Jellies belong to a group of animals with the scientific name Cnidaria, meaning "nettle," because many jellies and their relatives have a sting just like a nettle plant.

OUCH!

Jellies all have official scientific names, but most of them have common names too. These common names are like nicknames that really suit the particular kind of jelly.

▶ **Cauliflower jellyfish** have big, lumpy arms that look like fluffy cauliflower florets.

▶ When it's in the water, the **snotty jellyfish** is a regular jellyfish shape. But when it's washed up on the sand, all of its different body parts melt together into something that looks really disgusting—like a huge pool of slimy snot.

▶ **Fried egg jellyfish** have a golden yolky bump in their centers and a pale ring around their outsides that's like an egg white. Their texture is pretty similar to an egg, too—gelatinous and just a little bit rubbery.

▶ **Flower hat jellyfish** have a hat-shaped dome covered with brightly colored shapes and patterns.

FANCY!

SiZE MATTERS
FROM PEANUTS TO PIANOS

▶ **Irukandjis**, the world's smallest jellies, can be almost half an inch long—about the size of a peanut with the shell cracked off.

actual size

▶ **Lion's mane jellies**, the largest jellyfish in the world, can weigh up to nearly 2,200 pounds—the same as two grand pianos. They have thick masses of tentacles that look like a lion's shaggy mane.

ANCIENT JELLIES

Jellyfish fossils are some of the oldest animal fossils ever found. Many different kinds of marine animals appeared about 550 million years ago, and, before that, jellyfish may have had the open oceans pretty much to themselves. Sharing the oceans with hordes of other creatures doesn't seem to be cramping the jellies' style, though—they keep on multiplying and spreading at alarming rates.

RISE OF THE
MEGA JELLY

Portuguese man-of-war and **long stingy stringy thingies** (yes, they're both real animals!) might look like regular jellies, but they are both actually made up of heaps of different creatures—kind of like a bunch of children stacked up in a trench coat to disguise themselves as an adult. These creatures, which are called "zooids," work together like a single jelly. Each individual does a different job, including catching food, digesting it and defending the team against predators. These mega jellies can be enormous— more than 140 feet long, or about half as long as a football field.

UP CLOSE AND PERSONAL WITH . . .
A SEA WALNUT

Sea walnut seems like an unusual name for a jelly, right? But it suits this one perfectly. These jellies have small bodies covered in lumps and bumps, so they look an awful lot like walnuts. Also, they live in the sea. They've practically named themselves!

Sea walnuts begin laying eggs when they are just 13 days old, and pretty soon they're laying 10,000 eggs *every single day*. Obviously this keeps them pretty busy, but somehow they still find time to eat regular meals. Sea walnuts have seriously impressive appetites—they can eat more than ten times their own weight in food each day! They can double in size in a single day—all that food has to go somewhere.

Here's the really cool thing about these jellies—if you cut a sea walnut into pieces, you won't slow it down all that much. Each piece of gelatinous goop will grow into its own separate jellyfish, and they'll all be off living their own lives in just two or three days.

NO JOKE!

DON'T PEE ON ME!

Some jellies have powerful venom in their tentacles. **Irukandjis** are tiny, but they have a sting that is 1,000 times stronger than a tarantula bite! Even touching a little bit of **box jellyfish** tentacle can make you really sick, and if 15 feet of it touches your skin you might have only four minutes to live—or even two.

You might have heard that if a jelly stings you, someone should pee on the affected area to relieve the pain. You'll be happy to know there's no reason to ever get soaked in urine—this is definitely a myth. If you get stung you should seek immediate help from a doctor, but pouring vinegar over the area might help with the pain in the short term, depending on the type of jelly that stung you.

DO JELLYFISH LiVE FOREVER? THEY KIND OF DO, ACTUALLY.

R.I.P.

If jellyfish fall on hard times they have a secret power—they can "degrow." They shrink down to a tiny size so that they can eat a lot less food and still scrape by. When food is plentiful again, they grow back to their normal size. But that's not all jellies do to avoid death:

▶ **Moon jellies** can grow whole new body parts. They can also age backward, turning themselves back into baby jellies anytime they want. Imagine if humans could do those things!

▶ One kind of jellyfish literally lives forever. When it "dies" it begins to rot, which is pretty much what you expect from a dead body. But then something strange happens. Tiny parts of the rotting jelly find each other and come back together to form a baby jelly. All of this happens within five days of the "death," which is a pretty short timeframe in which to raise the dead. Their name won't surprise you— what else could you call them but **zombie jellies!**

▶ No one could call a jellyfish a quitter—lots of jellies keep on stinging even after death! They don't mean to sting things at this point, but their tentacles are still full of venom that will be released when touched.

CLIMATE CHANGE AND JELLIES

Climate change is bad news for just about everyone on the planet—but it may actually benefit jellyfish. This is because climate change will lead to oceans warming up. Warm water contains less oxygen—so some species will struggle to survive. But jellies don't need as much oxygen as other animals to breathe, so they'll be fine— tropical jellies (like those pesky and very poisonous **Irukandji**)

will likely spread further around the world.

Jellyfish might even have the ability to speed up climate change. Jellyfish make loads of carbon-rich feces and mucus (poo and goo) that bacteria use to breathe, which is just about the grossest thing ever. Not all bacteria are bad— some are really useful! But this particular kind produce a whole lot of carbon dioxide.

Jellyfish also eat vast numbers of things like plankton, which take a lot of carbon dioxide out of the atmosphere and oceans. Losing too much plankton will mean there's a lot more carbon dioxide in our oceans, which will speed up climate change.

WANT TO LEARN MORE ABOUT CLIMATE CHANGE? FLIP TO PAGE X!

SOLAR-POWERED JELLYFISH

On a small island in the Pacific Ocean, part of the island nation of Palau, swarms of **golden jellyfish** live in the aptly named Jellyfish Lake. These jellies follow the path of the sun as it moves through the sky each day, floating from one side of the lake to the other to make sure they stay in the sun's rays. But why do they do it? Not to get a tan, that's for sure! These particular jellies have a type of algae living in them that get their energy from the sun. The algae need the jellies to carry them around, so they supply the jellies with food and energy as a kind of trade for carrying them wherever the sun goes.

A GROUP OF JELLYFISH IS CALLED A SMACK. THEY CAN ALSO BE CALLED A BLOOM OR A SWARM.

SOUND THE ALARM!

Alarm jellyfish live deep in the ocean, where it's REALLY dark. Really dark, and also full of all kinds of weird creatures. A lot of these creatures have glowing lights to make living in the dark easier, and the alarm jelly is no different. But, unlike other glow-in-the-dark animals, this jelly doesn't use its lights to hunt. It uses them to avoid being eaten! When it's attacked, the alarm jellyfish launches into a dramatic performance with lots of flashing and spinning lights. This incredible show attracts a whole lot of other predators to the scene, which might seem like a bad idea. Surely hordes of dangerous predators are worse than just one, right? But there is logic behind the jelly's plan! It knows that all the new predators will probably go after the original attacker, giving the jelly a chance to escape.

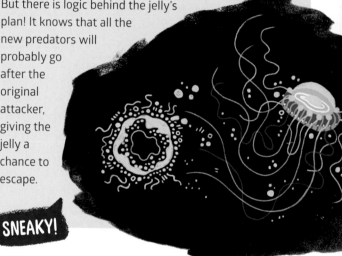

SNEAKY!

ARE JELLIES EVERYWHERE?

Jellies can thrive where few other species dare to go. Humans use scuba gear to breathe underwater, and some jellies use their body parts to do a similar thing! They absorb oxygen through their bells and hold on to it, kind of like taking a big gulp of air, which lets them swim into oxygen-less water without running out of breath.

Jellies can live pretty much anywhere in the ocean, but they don't just live in the salty water of the sea! A few tiny, stingless types of jelly can live in fresh water, too. So, yes, the world is pretty much bursting at the seams with jellies.

JELLYFISH v. EVERYONE

Jellies are cute, and the small ones look about as harmless as a shower cap. But don't be fooled! Jellies can cause a whole lot of trouble.

▶ Who would win—jellyfish or fishing boat? One average-sized jelly might not do much damage, but when a swarm of giant jellies is scooped up in a fishing net it can be heavy enough to tip an entire boat over. We're not talking about a tiny little dinghy, either—this once happened to a fishing trawler weighing 10 tons!

▶ Jellies are often sucked up with sea water into the cooling systems of nuclear power plants. Up to 150 tons of jellies are removed each day from some power plants just to keep them operating— that's millions of individual jellies sliming their way into machines and gunking them up until they stop working. Gross, but kind of impressive!

▶ In the Philippines, people were plunged into darkness one night when a huge swarm of jellies shut off the electricity! A large power plant had sucked up 50 truckloads of jellyfish through its cooling system, which shut off all the power and sent the plant into an actual blind panic— no one could see anything in the dark!

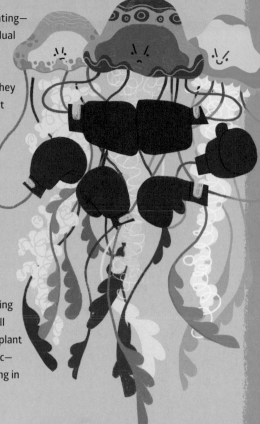

WHO'S HUNGRY?

Some jellies don't need to eat at all—they absorb tiny pieces of nutrient in the water through their skin. Most jellyfish don't try very hard to hunt for food—they just drift through the water, trailing their tentacles like nets to catch prey. But not all jellies are willing to wait for their food to come to them! When it comes to hunting, different species have their own special tricks.

▶ **Box jellyfish** are the only jellyfish with eyes and brains! They're wildly clever hunters that are able to get up some serious speed as they go after fish and crabs.

▶ **Australian spotted jellyfish** have a sneaky way of catching plankton. They shoot a special foam into the water to thicken it and make it harder for plankton to move around. Once the plankton are swimming in slow motion, the jellies glide in and gobble them up!

HOW DO THEY MOVE?

By pulsating their bells, some jellies can actively propel themselves through the water in a hypnotic movement. They actually pull themselves through the water, by creating a negative pressure in the water ahead of them, as they pulsate.

7

PIRANHAS

Piranha means "tooth fish" in Tupi, an indigenous language of Brazil. It's no surprise they were named after that particular feature—they have seriously fearsome grins. They live in freshwater lakes and rivers, including the Amazon River, and they can also commonly be found in the nightmares of people petrified of being eaten alive while swimming. True, piranhas are incredible hunters that are attracted to the smell of blood, but you'd be surprised at the things they'd choose to eat before sampling your toes!

SCAREDY FISH

Piranhas have huge teeth, but there are still plenty of larger, fiercer predators that can eat them, including caimans—relatives of alligators. Traveling in crowds makes them feel less open to attack—there's safety in numbers!

A FISH OR A DOG?

Red-bellied piranhas bark to frighten off predators.

WHERE CAN I SEE A PIRANHA?

Piranhas live in South America.

A GROUP OF PIRANHAS IS CALLED A SHOAL.

WHAT DOES A PIRANHA EAT?

Piranhas are known for having a taste for flesh, but plants are actually a common part of many piranhas' meals. Some of them are even vegetarian!

- Seeds, nuts, and riverweeds make tasty snacks for piranhas.

- Meaty prey commonly includes things like worms, crustaceans, snails, fish, and any dead animals or birds that they find in the water.

- If there isn't much food around, they can turn to cannibalism and start eating each other!

CAN A PIRANHA EAT ME?

A piranha certainly wouldn't turn its nose up at nibbling on human flesh, but the human would have to be dead or very close to it before piranhas made a proper meal of them. They generally only go after large prey such as humans or capybara if they're dead or severely injured. If there isn't a lot of other food around and you splash noisily into a piranha-infested river with a bleeding foot, you might be risking a piranha bite. That said, people regularly swim in rivers with piranhas without it turning into a bloodbath.

CRUNCH!

YUM!

FISH SCALES

Wimple piranhas swim quickly at their prey, barreling up and taking a firm bite before their hapless prey knows what's hit them. They aren't actually going after flesh, though—their favorite food is fish scales. They ram into fish to dislodge their scales, which they crunch down on as their frightened prey swims off (a few scales lighter!).

TEAMWORK MAKES THE DREAM WORK

Red-bellied piranhas are great at sharing! They look for food together, often lurking in underwater plants and waiting to spring out to surprise unsuspecting prey. When one fish comes across something meal-worthy they let the rest of the shoal know, and everyone gathers around to take turns tearing a mouthful out of their shared dinner. Piranha dinnertime isn't always so polite, though. These fish can go into a feeding frenzy when they're hungry and come across prey in the water, with masses of fish thrashing and flipping around to fight for a bite before their friends gobble it all down.

FROGS AND TOADS

Frogs and toads are more similar than you'd think. They're both amphibians and even share a scientific name, Anura, which means "without tail" in Latin. Anurans with smooth skin are usually called frogs, while ones with warty skin are usually called toads. But both smooth and warty-skinned types can occur within the one Anuran family. Frogs and toads are a lot more brutal than they look. Did you know there's a frog that can inject poison into its attackers using the horns on its head? Or one that breaks its own bones to use as weapons? And they're only the modern ones—ancient species were tough enough to tangle with baby dinosaurs!

WHERE CAN I SEE A FROG OR TOAD?

Frogs live on every continent except Antarctica.

A GROUP OF FROGS IS CALLED AN ARMY, A GROUP OF TOADS IS CALLED A KNOT.

BIG
AND SMALL

The smallest frog is the **Paedophryne amauensis**, which only grows up to one third of an inch long. The entire frog is the same size as a pea!

The largest frog is the **goliath frog**, which is about 1 foot long and can weigh more than 7 pounds—the same as a brand new human baby, but a whole lot slimier.

FLANNERY FILE

Some time ago I was working in a very remote village in New Guinea. One day, a woman brought in a gigantic frog and sat it down on the table in front of me. This frog was the size of a dinner plate! I thought maybe it was dead, because it was completely still. Then, with no warning, it leapt off the table and onto my chest! It got me right around the throat with its arms, kind of like a big frog-hug. Everyone in the village screamed—they thought I'd been attacked by this giant frog. But I couldn't stop laughing—the frog was just like a big baby. I picked it up and popped it back on the table, and it quickly bounded away.

THE PERFECT NAME

- ▶ **Rocket frogs** have a pointy nose that looks like the tip of a rocket ship—and they can launch like a rocket, too. The Australian rocket frog can jump 13 feet high!

- ▶ **Ornate Pac-Man frogs** have super-wide jaws, just like the famous yellow computer game character they are named after. They snap up their prey just as enthusiastically, too!

- ▶ **Venezuelan pebble toads** have bumpy, pebble-colored skin. When these tiny mountain-dwelling toads feel threatened they roll up and bounce away downhill just like a loose pebble.

- ▶ **Little devil frogs** are bright red, the same color as a cartoon of the devil, and they're packed full of poison, too.

- ▶ **Mossy frogs** have lumpy skin that is covered in mottled green patches. They look just like tiny, moss-covered rocks!

- ▶ **Glass frogs** have completely see-through skin, so when you're looking at them you can see all of the organs working away inside.

- ▶ **Wolverine frogs** are also known as hairy frogs or horror frogs. They have masses of hair-like growths sticking out near their back legs, a bit like Wolverine's shaggy sideburns. But that's not all! Just like the comic book character, these frogs have the ability to snap their own bones and force the bone spikes out through the skin of their feet to protect themselves. Once they've neutralized the threat they pull the broken bones back inside their bodies and start to heal. **INCREDIBLE!**

FROG FOOD

Tadpoles can eat plants, but mature frogs and toads are carnivorous. They'll eat just about any insect or animal that will fit inside their mouths, including larger prey such as mice, fish, other frogs, and even small snakes. That's pretty brave!

Why do frogs blink so much as they eat? Well, frogs can push their eyes so far back into their heads as they blink that their eyeballs help push the food down their throats. **WILD!**

EGG ADVENTURES

Frogs and toads often lay their eggs straight into the water, but sometimes they lay them on part of a plant that's hanging over a body of water instead. When these tadpoles hatch they slither off the plant and into the water below. **NIFTY!**

▶ In Japan, the female **forest green tree frog** produces a fluid similar to egg whites, which she whips into a thick foam using her back legs. She makes a large, baseball-sized sphere of foam that will hold all her eggs securely up in a tree until they're ready to hatch.

▶ Frog eggs look like a tasty snack to many animals, but **red-eyed tree frog** eggs aren't quite as helpless as they look. If they sense a predator, the tiny tadpoles start to wriggle furiously inside their eggs. They release a special chemical that helps them break through the egg wall, letting them hatch early and dive into the water below.

CLIMATE CHANGE

Changes to the temperature of their homes or to water levels can make it much harder for frogs and toads to survive. The **golden toad** of Costa Rica may have already been driven extinct by the changing climate.

IS BEING A TADPOLE COMPULSORY?

Surinam toads skip the tadpole stage altogether—they pop out of their eggs fully formed. Mothers lay up to 100 eggs at a time, which settle onto their flat, broad backs and become embedded in the skin. When they're ready to hatch, the baby toads tear holes in the skin and burst through! Luckily the holes heal over afterwards.

CAN A FROG KILL YOU?

Frogs are pretty cute, so you might think there's no way they could be dangerous. But you'd be wrong! Not only are some frogs poisonous, but some are toxic enough to kill you.

▸ The **golden poison dart frog** has enough poison to **DEADLY!** kill ten adult humans.

▸ Some frogs don't make their own poison—instead, they eat a range of toxic insects and reuse their poison for their own protection.

▸ Many poisonous frogs are brightly colored and have elaborate patterns. These colors work as a warning to predators, who know that brightly colored frogs are likely to give them a nasty surprise (i.e., pain and death) if they try to eat them.

▸ **Greening's frogs** have spiky growths on their skulls that they use to inject their poison instead of waiting for it to absorb through the skin.

FLANNERY FILE

I was once camped in the desert in Central Australia during a thunderstorm. There was lots of thunder before any rain fell, and I heard frogs calling from the bone-dry sand dune I was camped on. You might think deserts are too dry for frogs to live in, but some species bury themselves in the sand and rest for long periods until it rains. The frogs I heard must have been roused from their slumber by the sound of the thunder. By morning enough rain had fallen to create a lake at the foot of the dune, and it was completely full of frogs!

ANCIENT DINOSAUR-EATERS

Frogs and toads have been around in some form or another for more than 200 million years. The fossilized bones of one ancient species were found in Madagascar. The species has been given the name **devil frog** or "devil frog from hell." This frog lived about 70 million years ago and was a large, aggressive predator that may have even eaten baby dinosaurs!

WHALES

Whales can grow to sizes that are, quite frankly, very intimidating. Don't let that scare you, though—even though they're the biggest animals in the ocean, most whales enjoy chomping down on teeny-tiny prey such as krill. They have excellent singing voices, strangely useful poop, and a whole heap of weird body parts—including giant heads, forehead teeth, and, if you go back far enough in history, legs.

SEASONED TRAVELERS

Gray whales have the longest migration of any mammal. They travel an astounding 10,000 miles each year between their summer feeding grounds near Alaska and their breeding grounds near the coast of Mexico.

WHERE CAN I SEE A WHALE?

Whales travel a lot to find the right climate for feeding and mating, so they can be seen anywhere from the freezing cold waters around the Arctic and Antarctic to tropical coastal areas.

A GROUP OF WHALES iS CALLED A POD (OR A GAM, PLUMP, OR HERD).

DIVING CHAMPS

Sperm whales can dive more than 3,000 feet deep in the ocean to look for giant squid, holding their breath for up to an hour and a half at a time. Their remarkable diving abilities might have something to do with a mysterious substance called "spermaceti." Their heads are packed full of the stuff, which is thought to help these whales adjust their ability to either float or sink in the water.

IS THAT A UNICORN?

Male **narwhals** have a giant spike sticking out the front of their heads. They're the big, blubbery unicorns of the sea! Despite looking like a horn, narwhals' spikes are actually ridiculously long teeth. This special forehead tooth can grow to more than 8 feet long, but scientists aren't sure why they grow that way. Maybe it's to attract a mate, or to use as a weapon—either way, they look pretty magical.

HUGE HEADS v. BIG BRAINS

Right whales have particularly huge heads—they take up one third of their entire bodies! They don't have the biggest brains, though—that award goes to **sperm whales**, which have bigger brains than any other animal in the world.

SINGING STARS

Whales can be incredibly loud! **Toothed whales** and **baleen whales** make different kinds of sounds, and they make them for different reasons, too:

▶ Toothed whales make a range of clicks, whistles, clangs, and groans. These noises help them communicate with each other and find their way around in the ocean. Their clicking sounds travel long distances through the water, bouncing off anything in their paths, including things like fish and rocks, and ricocheting back to the whale. When the altered sounds come back the whale can work out what they've bounced off—it's like they're mapping the ocean around them using sound.

▶ Many baleen whales, including male **blue whales** and **bowhead whales**, are known for singing complex and incredibly beautiful songs. Male **humpback whales** have some of the most famous whale songs. They're also the loudest animals in the world! Other whales can hear their songs from thousands of miles away. The reason whales sing is shrouded in mystery, but it is likely to be related to mating.

SLEEPING STANDING UP

Sperm whales don't need a whole lot of sleep—only about seven minutes at a time. They usually nap near the surface of the ocean, floating completely vertically!

SPA DAY

Bowhead and **beluga whales** use rocks to exfoliate! They rub up against rough rocks to get rid of the layers of dead skin that build up on their bodies. They'll even go out of their way to reach certain rocky outcrops that are effective exfoliants, traveling long distances just to have a good scrub.

SNOT STUDIES

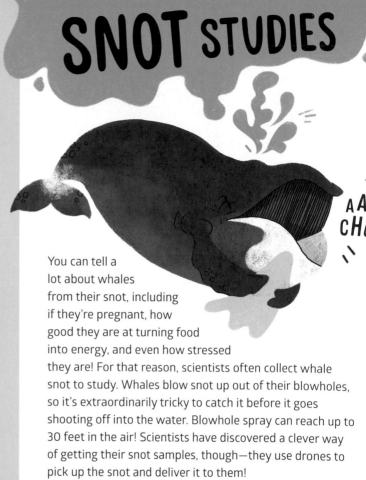

AAA CHOO

You can tell a lot about whales from their snot, including if they're pregnant, how good they are at turning food into energy, and even how stressed they are! For that reason, scientists often collect whale snot to study. Whales blow snot up out of their blowholes, so it's extraordinarily tricky to catch it before it goes shooting off into the water. Blowhole spray can reach up to 30 feet in the air! Scientists have discovered a clever way of getting their snot samples, though—they use drones to pick up the snot and deliver it to them!

A DENTIST'S DREAM

Some whales have teeth, others have baleen. What's the difference?

▶ Whale baleen looks like big furry combs inside their jaws. Baleen is made of the same thing as your hair and fingernails, only on a much larger scale—whales have hundreds of plates of baleen in their mouths, and each piece can be nearly 8 feet long. That means each plate is almost definitely taller than either of your parents! They eat by gulping huge mouthfuls of water, then letting the water drain out. As the water drains, the baleen catches the krill, plankton and tiny fish for the whale to gobble down.

DELICIOUS!

Scientists recently discovered that these kinds of whales have a weird organ buried in their chins. It looks like a jelly blob with fingers, and it helps them judge when they have taken in enough water to sieve through their baleen.

▶ Whales without baleen generally have sharp, pointed teeth, which means they can eat bigger prey like fish, squid, and crabs. But they don't do a whole lot of chewing—they mostly use their teeth to hook onto their prey, which they then swallow whole.

My first job as director of the South Australian Museum was to arrange an expedition to collect a rare, gigantic **southern right whale** skeleton. The museum curator led a team to the beach where the dead whale had washed up. As soon as she arrived, she put on her rubber boots and waterproof pants and waded right into the whale's rotting body so she could cut the remaining flesh off the bones. But just as she got inside the whale's skeleton, a huge wave came up and pulled the carcass out into the water. It was quickly surrounded by a pack of six great white sharks that started feeding on the whale meat. Everyone thought, *Oh no! She'll be eaten alive!* But, luckily, the next wave washed her and the carcass back onto the shore. Even after she'd been washed back up, she didn't abandon the job. It was stinky and gross and scary, but she didn't care! She was so passionate about getting this skeleton back to the museum.

Once all of the bones had been collected, the team loaded them into the museum truck and drove back to the city. That afternoon, I got a very angry phone call from someone saying, "I'm going to sue the museum for damage to my car!" I thought, *What on EARTH? How can this day get any weirder?!* He said, "I was driving behind your museum truck and something was leaking out. It's stripped all the paint off my car!" The heat had melted the oil in the whale bones, and it had dripped out of the truck and splattered onto this poor guy's car. The oil was so powerful, it stripped the paint clean off! We had to pay to fix his car, of course.

WHALE MILK

Baby whales grow up fast. Newborn **blue whales** can gain 200 pounds a day for the first part of their lives! Part of the reason they grow so astronomically quickly is that whale milk is super fatty—human milk is about 4 percent fat, while whale milk is more like 40 percent fat! Their milk is also extraordinarily thick—almost like toothpaste.

A WHALE WITH LEGS?

Whales didn't always live in the ocean—their ancient relatives originally lived on land! One of the earliest types of whale was called **Pakicetus**, and these ancient mammals had four legs and sharp teeth. They were much smaller than modern whales—more like the size of a wolf. They moved into the sea and lost their legs about 50 million years ago.

THE BIGGEST ANIMAL EVER

A WHALE OF A TIME

Most whales live well beyond the average human lifespan—**bowhead whales** can live for up to 200 years!

A FRESH LOOK

Belugas, also known as **white whales**, aren't actually born white. They become white after about five years—before that, they're gray or brown.

The largest whale is the **blue whale**. These ocean giants can grow to more than 100 feet long, which is about one third the length of a football field. They can weigh as much as 220 tons—as much as a house! They are the biggest animals to EVER live on Earth (including the dinosaurs).

The smallest whale is the **dwarf sperm whale**. The biggest ones weigh about 660 pounds, which isn't even half the weight of a cow, and the longest are up to 9 feet.

CLIMATE CHANGE

A warming planet means melting ice in the polar regions, which actually makes it easier for some whales, like **humpbacks** and **bowheads**, to find food. As the water warms they can stay for longer in their colder feeding grounds. But carbon dioxide is affecting the acidity levels in the ocean, which will continue to affect the availability of whale food—krill won't do so well in more acidic waters.

FLANNERY FILE

I once went out in a canoe into the tropical sea north of Bali to look for whales. It was a still, quiet morning, the sea as still as glass. We saw a serrated shape ahead and paddled carefully towards it, and it turned out that there were two **sperm whales** resting at the ocean's surface, as well as half a dozen dolphins cavorting around them. We drifted until we were really close. Then one of the whales slowly arched its back, raising its tail high above our heads as it slid gracefully into the sea. The second whale followed, and our canoe was left alone on the vastness of the ocean.

POOP AND PEE

- Among other things, **blue whales** eat krill. Krill eat tiny life forms called "phytoplankton," which need iron to grow. Blue whales have a lot of iron in their poop, so every time they poop more phytoplankton bloom in the water. That leads to more krill, which means more tasty snacks for the whales. So they're attracting food just by pooping, and then as they eat they poop even more. It's a beautiful (though stinky) cycle!

- It is hard to measure how much whales pee—they live in the water, so any pee spreads out around them pretty quickly—but one study suggested that **fin whales** release 257 gallons of pee *each day*. That could fill up four bathtubs! Every now and then whales can be seen lying on their backs and letting a plume of pee burst upward like a fountain.

A HEALTHY APPETITE

Whales don't get to be as big as they are by picking at their food—in fact, they eat almost constantly. **Sperm whales** munch down about 1,000 pounds of fish and squid each day, and **blue whales** can eat more than 7,500 pounds of krill over the same period of time.

IMPRESSIVE!

I'LL *RACE* YOU!

Male **humpback whales** get wildly competitive when it comes to mating, racing against each other in something called a "heat run." During a heat run, up to 40 males will compete for one female. She sets off at a fast pace with a horde of males thrashing along behind her. The males noisily flap their tails and fins against the water to intimidate each other, jostling to get closest to the female. When they really get going the males begin to collide with each other, and leap out of the water onto one another. As you can imagine, a fully grown humpback whale crashing down on you can really slow you down!

OTTERS

Otters are aquatic members of the weasel family, and they can live either in the ocean or in fresh water. Otter dads don't usually stick around for long, so moms and their babies live together—and they make ridiculously cute families. Go ahead and look at pictures of otters holding hands—you'll agree. Otters love going down waterslides as much as the average kid, and they're really into brushing their fur. Really, REALLY into it. Read on to find out why otters carry rocks around and what the deal is with their poo.

WHERE CAN I SEE AN OTTER?

Otters live in waterways on every continent except for Antarctica and Australia. Sea otters live along the coast of the Pacific Ocean in North America and Asia.

SEA OTTERS PLAY WITH ROCKS, THROWING AND CATCHING A NUMBER OF THEM IN THE AIR, KIND OF LIKE JUGGLING.

A GROUP OF OTTERS ON LAND IS CALLED A ROMP, BUT IN THE WATER A GROUP IS CALLED A RAFT.

DINNERTIME!

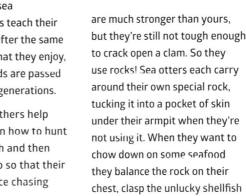

All otters are carnivores. **Sea otters** eat things like squid, fish, crabs, and sea urchins. **River otters** eat things like frogs, crabs, fish, and crayfish. Most otters can eat up to 15 percent of their body weight each day, but **California sea otters** eat on a whole other level—they can eat up to 25 to 35 percent.

▸ River otters have long, sensitive whiskers that pick up on tiny movements in the water, helping the otters to sense nearby food.

▸ Sea otters have favorite foods, just like you. Well, not just like you—unless you enjoy eating black snails or sea urchins. Parents teach their children to go after the same types of food that they enjoy, so favorite foods are passed down through generations.

▸ River otter mothers help their pups learn how to hunt by catching fish and then letting them go so that their pup can practice chasing them down.

▸ Sea otters really enjoy eating shellfish and clams. Their teeth are much stronger than yours, but they're still not tough enough to crack open a clam. So they use rocks! Sea otters each carry around their own special rock, tucking it into a pocket of skin under their armpit when they're not using it. When they want to chow down on some seafood they balance the rock on their chest, clasp the unlucky shellfish in their paws and smash it over and over again into the rock until it cracks open. **GENIUS!**

There are 13 different types of otter. Numbers are shrinking for nearly all of them—the **North American river otter** is one type that is doing really well. Five species of otter have been classified as endangered. One of the reasons otters are struggling is their history of being hunted by humans for their fur.

13 OTTERS TO LOVE

1. **Sea otter** ENDANGERED

2. **European otter** (Eurasian otter)

3. **Hairy-nosed otter** (this one was thought to be extinct for a while) ENDANGERED

4. **Spotted-necked otter** (speckle-throated otter)

5. **Smooth-coated otter**

6. **North American river otter**

7. **Southern American river otter** (large river otter) ENDANGERED

8. **Amazonian river otter** (long-tailed otter)

9. **Giant otter** ENDANGERED

10. **Asian small-clawed otter**

11. **African clawless otter** (African small-clawed otter)

12. **Congo clawless otter**

13. **Marine otter** ENDANGERED

21

TOUGH GUYS

Groups of otters can gang up and make loud calls to scare off predators. They might not look scary, but **river otters** have been recorded frightening off jaguars!

BUILT TO SWIM

Sea otters occasionally come onto land to rest and **river otters** sleep in burrows called "holts" and sometimes hang out on land, but all otters spend a lot of time in the water. They have a whole host of features that make swimming a breeze.

▶ Otter feet have webbing, kind of like built-in flippers to help them swim.

▶ Otter ears and noses can close off in the water so that they don't get clogged up with water when they're diving.

▶ The broad, powerful tail of an otter is called a "rudder," which helps otters push through the water like an extra limb.

▶ Otters have powerful lungs that allow them to hold their breath underwater for up to eight minutes. **IMPRESSIVE!**

▶ Otters have two layers of incredibly thick fur—a layer of short fur underneath and a second layer of long fur on top. Their fur traps air close to their skin, keeping it warm and dry even as they're swimming in icy water.

SWIMMING LESSONS

All otter babies can naturally float as soon as they're born—they bob around in the water like a cork—but they can't swim right away. Luckily baby otters don't take long to learn how to swim—after a couple of lessons from their mothers they're zipping around like pros.

HOW BIG IS AN OTTER?

The **giant otter**, as its name suggests, is the largest otter. It grows up to almost 5 feet, 11 inches, which is taller than many adult humans! It's not the heaviest otter, though—that award goes to the **sea otter**, which can weigh up to 90 pounds.

The smallest otter is the **Asian small-clawed otter**. These little critters only weigh 11 pounds at the most—about half the weight of a wiener dog. They're short, too, only growing to about 3 feet long.

STICKING TOGETHER

While their babies are still learning how to swim, otter mothers have to make sure their little ones don't float off down the river or across the waves. They have a few ingenious (and adorable) ways of keeping tabs on them:

▶ Otter mothers float on their backs, clasping their baby in their arms on top of their bellies.

▶ Mother and baby pairs can both float on their backs together, holding paws to make sure they don't get separated by the current.

▶ **Sea otters** sometimes bundle their babies up in floating masses of seaweed so they can go and hunt without their baby drifting off!

MESSAGES IN THE POOP

Otter poo has a special name—it's called "spraint," and otters are very particular about it. Like humans, they don't poo just anywhere— they have a designated spot for it. Otters can tell a lot about each other by sniffing piles of poop, including how old another otter is and what sex they are. Taking a big whiff of poo sounds like a pretty gross way to get to know someone, but some people think otter poop actually smells quite nice—like jasmine tea or freshly mown hay! Not everyone agrees on that point, though— others think it stinks like rotting fish. If you ever come across some otter poo, give it a sniff and see what you think!

EW!

DOLPHINS

Picture a dolphin. You're probably thinking of a sleek gray creature frolicking off the coast of a tropical island. Maybe one with a cute smile and a sweet, chirruping call. Well, you're right—many dolphins are just like that! But did you know that dolphins also live in freshwater rivers? Or that **melon-headed whales** and **orcas**, also known as **killer whales**, are actually both types of dolphin? Dolphins are full of surprises—and they have some deeply weird habits.

WHERE CAN I SEE A DOLPHIN?

River dolphins live in freshwater rivers in South America and Asia. **Ocean dolphins** live all around the world. Many dolphins prefer warmer coastal waters, but even the colder and deeper parts of the ocean have dolphin residents, including the mighty **orca**.

A GROUP OF DOLPHINS IS CALLED A POD.

SURF BROS

Dolphins like to surf! They use their bodies to catch waves, including the waves caused by boats as they cut through the water.

RAD!

WHAT'S SO GOOD ABOUT
SEA SPONGES?

Sea sponges are big lumps of sponge that grow in the ocean. They might not sound exciting to you, but dolphins love them!

- ▶ Male **humpback dolphins** have been seen giving sea sponges as gifts to females they like. It's the dolphin version of giving your crush a bunch of roses.

- ▶ The **bottlenose dolphins** from Shark Bay in Australia have some weird habits. They tear off pieces of sea sponge and stick them over their snouts. As far as fashion goes, this might look a little questionable, but the dolphins aren't doing it to be cute. They use their snouts to seek out food on the rough surface of the ocean floor, and the sponges stop their noses from getting scratched and damaged. **CLEVER!**

RIVER
DWELLERS

Some ocean-dwelling dolphins can occasionally venture into fresh water, but there are only a handful of species of dolphin that live exclusively in fresh water. They have more flexible necks than ocean dolphins, allowing them to turn sharply to avoid obstacles. They can also swim upside down! The life of a **river dolphin** isn't all fun and games, though—pollution, hunting, and construction are making it harder and harder for these creatures to survive.

SHARK
ATTACK

Sharks attack and eat dolphins, but these powerful predators are regularly thwarted by clever pods of dolphins that don't want to become dinner.

- ▶ Dolphins are much more agile in the water than sharks. They have the ability to swim steeply up and down, while sharks swim best going forward. That makes it much easier for dolphins to evade capture.

- ▶ Pods of dolphins gang up to scare away sharks. They're fearless in a fight, ducking in and beating the shark with their tails to frighten it away.

- ▶ Sometimes dolphins will swim up underneath a shark to attack its soft underbelly, hitting it with their snouts. It doesn't seem like a nose jab would do that much damage, but a dolphin snout is strong enough to stun a shark, or even kill it.

BABY
MUSTACHE

Imagine if you were born with a beard. Well, that's almost the reality for baby dolphins. They're born almost completely hairless except for a row of hairs across their snout, like a baby mustache, which falls out after about a week.

HITCHING A RIDE

Baby dolphins can't swim very well at first, but they have a nifty trick to help them keep up with their super-speedy mothers. By swimming right up close to their mom, they get sucked into her slipstream. They barely have to work to keep up; they can just relax and get pulled along.

LAZY?

OR INSPIRED?

GOING FOR A SPIN

Dolphins are famous for their graceful leaps out of the water. **Spinning dolphins** and **spotted dolphins** are particularly high jumpers—they can reach over 15 feet in the air! Spinning dolphins do something a little special as they leap—as their name suggests, they spin like ballet dancers! They start spinning under the water to build up power, and then burst up into the air, where they keep spinning. They can make seven full turns in just one second before crashing back down into the water.

SPITTING

Snubfin dolphins don't spit their food out, they spit *at* their food! They hunt in groups, spitting powerful jets of water to herd fish together so they can catch them more easily.

FLANNERY FILE

Once I was filming a documentary in Australia's Shark Bay, and we saw a pod of wild dolphins quite a long way from the shore. I swam out toward them, and they didn't move away. In fact, one of them came right up over my shoulder! I had a GoPro camera with me, so I took a selfie with the dolphin resting its head on my shoulder.

TERRIBLE TABLE MANNERS

Dolphins don't really chew their food—despite having sharp teeth, they have quite weak jaw muscles. That doesn't stop them from eating, though! They use their teeth to grab onto their prey, which they usually swallow whole.

Sometimes dolphins shake their food or rub it against a rough surface to break it into pieces. Imagine if you tried eating like that at the dinner table! **Bottlenose dolphins** sometimes beat cuttlefish to get rid of their ink, or scrape them along the ocean floor to remove their bony parts. They've also been observed removing the heads of catfish before eating them to avoid being poked by their sharp spines.

THE NEWEST DOLPHINS

Only three new species of dolphin have been discovered since the 2000s. The **Burrunan dolphin**, living around the coast near Melbourne, in Australia, was recognized as a new species in 2011. Other new additions to the dolphin gang are the **snubfin dolphin**, discovered in 2005 in New Guinea, and the **Australian humpback dolphin**, in 2014. A case was put forward in 2014 for a new type of river dolphin living in Brazil, called the **Araguaian boto**. But scientists can't agree if this dolphin is a close relative of the **Amazon river dolphin** or part of the same species.

SOUND MAPS

Many dolphins use echolocation to find food and map out their surroundings. They make up to 1,000 clicking sounds per second, and these sounds travel through the ocean and collide with objects or other animals, sending back echoes to the dolphin to let them know what is nearby. The messages these echoes pass on to the dolphin are amazingly detailed—they can find out how far away things are, how big they are, and what shape they are.

DOLPHIN TO THE RESCUE!

Dolphins are known for being remarkably compassionate. If one of their group is injured they will help it up to the water's surface so it can breathe, and they even come to the rescue of other animals. Moko, a **bottlenose dolphin**, famously helped rescue two pygmy sperm whales that were stranded on a New Zealand beach. Humans had been trying to rescue them for some time, but the whales kept washing back onto the sand. Moko swam up and helped guide them away from the beach and out into open water.

WHAT A HERO!

MODERN FAMILIES

Male **orcas** don't raise their own babies. After mating, they leave their partner and move back to live with their mothers! That might sound a little irresponsible, but male orcas are actually very helpful in other ways. They're really good at babysitting their younger relatives, often helping to look after their nieces, nephews, and younger siblings. Many other dolphins, including **bottlenose dolphins**, live in larger pods where everyone helps take care of any babies in the group.

DID YOU SAY MY NAME?

Each **bottlenose dolphin** has its own signature whistle that helps the pod communicate and keep track of each other. The whistles are like names— dolphins use their whistle to identify themselves, and if they hear another dolphin call it out, they'll respond.

ORCAS ON THE HUNT

Orcas are apex predators, so they spend most of their time thinking of ingenious ways to catch food instead of worrying about being eaten. They often live in cooler parts of the ocean, with plenty of ice around, and different clans specialize in catching different types of food. Some eat only salmon, and others only seals—a bit like the way some people like toast for breakfast and others prefer cereal.

- Orcas often work in groups to take down prey, such as seals. They don't settle for gobbling up the ones swimming in the water—they go after the ones on the ice, too. They splash water over chunks of ice floating on the ocean surface to wash the hapless seals off, or dive underneath the floes and knock them from below to make them tilt or even split apart.

- Even whales aren't safe from orcas. One of the ways they overpower such enormous prey is flopping on top of them—weighing them down in the water to tire them out. It's a bit like an older sibling sitting on you so you can't run off; only in that case, you don't end up being eaten!

BEST FRIENDS

Male **bottlenose dolphins** form lifelong friendships, and often bond closely with one or two others, working together to impress females. These bonded dolphins are often seen swimming side by side, jumping through the air in unison, rubbing against each other, and overlapping the fins on the sides of their bodies—a bit like holding hands.

SWEET!

PUFFERFISH

Pufferfish have huge eyes and big, full fish lips, but don't let their cuteness fool you! These sweet-looking fish have a surprisingly large number of ways to cause discomfort and even death for anything that tries to eat them. You can find them in oceans and fresh water, nibbling on some shocking things and getting all puffed out of shape when someone bothers them.

HOW BIG IS A PUFFERFISH?

The **dwarf pufferfish** is about 1 inch long, or the width of a one-dollar coin. You could hold a whole handful of them at once, but you probably shouldn't!

WHERE CAN I SEE A PUFFERFISH?

Pufferfish prefer warmer waters, especially tropical parts of the ocean. They sometimes live in subtropical waters, and even venture into fresh water, but never cold water.

PUFFERFISH CAN SWIM BACKWARD AS WELL AS FORWARD —A VERY RARE SKILL FOR A FISH.

TOE BITERS

One type of pufferfish, **ferocious pufferfish**, has been known to bite. Its teeth are so powerful that they can tear off large chunks of human flesh, usually out of people's feet.

YUCK!

BACK OFF

Pufferfish aren't great at swimming, which is unfortunate for an animal that lives in water. Luckily, they have a lot of other cool skills to make up for it!

- When they sense danger, pufferfish swell up to enormous sizes. They don't hold their breath to do it—they suck in large amounts of water, and can still breathe even when they look like balloons. If a pufferfish inflates after it's been seized by a predator, it can block up the attacker's throat and make it impossible to breathe—it's not giving up without a fight!

- Pufferfish don't have scales—they're covered in tough skin instead, which can change color to help them blend into their environment.

- Lots of species of pufferfish are covered in spines, but they mostly lie flat against their bodies. The spines can be hard to spot until the fish puff up—then they're impossible to miss!

- Many pufferfish are chock-full of a poison called "tetrodotoxin." One pufferfish can be poisonous enough to kill five ice hockey teams—that's 30 people! The poison starts by making your lips and tongue go numb, then your entire body gradually becomes paralyzed before you eventually die. This poison is super toxic to most other animals, too—only a few sharks are able to snack on a pufferfish and live to tell the tale.

UNDERWATER ARTISTS

White-spotted pufferfish males go to a lot of effort to find a mate. They spend about a week working 24 hours a day to build an elaborate nest on the sandy ocean floor. The nests look like a work of art—they're shaped like a sunburst, with peaks and valleys of sand radiating out from a circular center. The male fish builds these shapes by wriggling through the sand, and even decorates his masterpiece with carefully collected pieces of shell and coral! After finding a mate, the male stays in his nest until the eggs hatch, then he abandons it! The male only uses each nest once before moving on to build a fresh nest for a whole new set of eggs.

THAT'S DEDICATION!

BOYS AND GIRLS

Dwarf pufferfish are not born male or female—they take on a sex later in life. If they become male they are able to release a special hormone into the water that makes sure other pufferfish living nearby become female—that way, they can become the alpha male with no competition.

CRABS

Crabs are crustaceans, relatives of lobsters and prawns. You're probably familiar with them—you might have seen one of these eight-legged creatures scurrying along a beach, or a cartoon version singing about living under the sea in *The Little Mermaid*. There are more than 4,500 different species of crab, though, and not all of them are ocean-dwellers. Many crabs live on land, and some even live in trees!

WOULD YOU CUDDLE A CRAB?

Some crabs, including **teddy bear crabs** and **orangutan crabs**, have luscious locks across their bodies. They might look soft and fuzzy from the outside, but don't be fooled—there's still a hard shell and two snapping claws underneath all that fluff!

A GROUP OF CRABS iS CALLED A CAST

(NOT THE KiND YOU PUT ON A BROKEN ARM, OBViOUSLY).

ON THE HUNT

Some crabs eat meat, others eat plants. They have a number of ingenious methods for finding their dinner:

▸ **Soldier crabs** hunt together in large troops, clearing out every speck of food hidden on a beach, one section at a time. The smooth beach becomes covered in tiny bumps of displaced sand as they dig for food.

▸ **Pea crabs** are tiny, pea-sized crabs that live inside the shells of creatures like oysters, mussels, and clams. They don't need to hunt—when food filters into the shell of their host, the sneaky little crab steals it!

▸ **Sand bubbler crabs** eat by shoving sand into their mouths with their claws. They eat tiny bits of food from between the grains, spitting out the leftover sand and rolling it into a ball that they throw behind them as they move. And they move fast! At low tide they quickly comb through the sand and then bury themselves beneath it so that the waves don't sweep them away.

THE SPIDER AND THE PEA

Not all crabs are the cute little critters you see scurrying around on the beach—the **Japanese spider crab** has a leg span of more than 13 feet! To put that in perspective, the tallest human to ever live was 8 feet, 11 inches. That's SERIOUSLY big. Japanese spider crabs live for up to 100 years, so they have plenty of time for growing. The tiniest crab species is the **pea crab**. As the name suggests, these crabs can be as small as a quarter of an inch, or about the size of a pea.

EXTRA ARMOR

Carrier crabs, also called "urchin crabs," have hard shells like most other crabs. But they aren't content with their built-in armor—they want extra protection! They pick up things like sea urchins, rocks, and shells from the ocean floor and carry them around on their backs like a shield, often choosing poisonous urchins with vicious spikes. The urchins don't seem to mind—they get carried to new places where they can find food—but it does mean the crabs only have four legs left to walk with. The other four are busy clinging on to their shield!

TWO TUMMIES

WOW!

Crabs have two stomachs, and one of them has teeth inside it! Because they don't have any teeth inside their mouths, crabs need a toothy stomach to help them break down the chunks of food they swallow before passing it on to the second stomach to complete the act of digestion.

33

GIMME A C!

The **pom-pom crab** has tiny little claws, but you barely notice the size of them—you're too busy staring at the miniature pom-poms it's clasping like a crabby cheerleader. The pom-poms are actually sea anemones, which the crabs use to ward off predators. If they lose one of their pom-poms these crabs do something pretty brutal—they tear the remaining one in two! Luckily the sea anemones are very hardy, and regenerate into two whole anemones quite quickly. The crabs sweeten the deal by sharing some of their leftover food with their claw decorations, so it's not all bad.

UP CLOSE AND PERSONAL WITH . . . A CHRISTMAS ISLAND RED CRAB

As their name suggests, these crabs live on Christmas Island—and their shells are an eye-catching red.

▶ These flashy crabs eat mostly plants, rifling through leaf litter on the forest floor to find snacks.

▶ They live on land, but they still need to keep their gills moist so they can breathe. That means no basking in the sun! They avoid the heat by hanging out in the shade and digging burrows to sleep in. During the hottest part of the year they spend up to three months in their burrows, even blocking up the doorways so they don't dry out inside.

▶ Adult crabs live on land, but their babies spend their first month or so in the ocean. That means that when the crabs are ready to start their families, they need to head to the beach. They choose when to go based on when the tide is highest, which means millions of crabs flood out of the forest and toward the ocean at once. As you can imagine, seeing hordes of bright red crabs on the move is pretty incredible, and these crabs aren't shy about making a spectacle. Over a couple of weeks they tramp across roads in waves, scaling cliffs, and even venturing into houses on their way to the ocean. It's pandemonium!

DESERT DWELLERS

Inland freshwater crabs make their home in very dry parts of Australia. During heatwaves or long periods of drought, they dig deep burrows in the earth where they can keep cool and live off their stores of fat until the rains arrive. They can keep this up for an impressive six years!

TREE CLIMBERS

SOME CRABS LiVE ON LAND AND SOME LiVE iN WATER, BUT THERE ARE A FEW ADVENTUROUS TYPES THAT WANT TO BE UP iN THE TREES!

▶ The *Kani maranjandu* lives in the hollows of trees in India, using its slender, sharp-tipped legs to scamper around on the bark. Like many other land-dwelling crabs, it needs to keep its gills wet so it can breathe—it does it by dipping them into pools of rainwater that collect in tree hollows.

▶ **Coconut crabs** live on land, but regularly climb trees to cut down coconuts, which they are able to crack with their extraordinarily powerful claws. These monster crabs can weigh more than 8 pounds and stretch to 3 feet wide. As well as feasting on coconuts, they've been known to hunt birds! They clamber up into trees, latch on to their unlucky prey, and tear them apart, using their powerful claws to crunch through their bones with ease.

FLANNERY FILE

Christmas Island, off the northwest coast of Australia, is a kingdom of crabs! There are hardly any other large kinds of land animals living on the island, but you can see **red crabs**, **blue crabs**, and **coconut crabs** everywhere! There are tens of millions of them. I went to a local school where the janitor had begun to feed leftover lunch scraps to the coconut crabs living behind it. I went to take a look and found myself standing among the rocks with hundreds of gigantic coconut crabs milling around and waiting for food. These crabs can be enormous, and they look a bit like giant spiders.

SPOOKY!

WARRIOR CRABS

Some crabs have dips and creases across the surface of their shells that look uncannily like human faces. The **heikegani crab** from Japan is sometimes called the "samurai crab," because many people think their shells look like the faces of fierce samurai warriors.

WHERE CAN I SEE A CRAB?

Crabs can be found in oceans all around the world. Some crabs also live on land or in fresh water, and these crabs generally prefer warmer, tropical countries.

SEAHORSES

Seahorses' faces look distinctly horsey, hence the name. Despite their odd likeness to large hoofed creatures, seahorses are in fact a type of fish. Seahorse babies, which are truly tiny, are called "fry," giving everyone the perfect opportunity to use the expression "small fry" in a completely correct scientific context. Seahorses are laughably bad swimmers, especially considering they're fish, but they make up for it by being really good at playing hide-and-seek.

WHERE CAN I SEE A SEAHORSE?

Seahorses are usually found in warm and shallow coastal waters around the world, although a few types live in slightly cooler waters off the coast of places like Ireland, England, and Japan.

A GROUP OF SEAHORSES iS CALLED A HERD.

DROPPING ANCHOR

Seahorses rely on their remarkably flexible tails to stay anchored. They curl them around seagrass, coral, or anything else they can get a solid grip on so that their delicate bodies don't get buffeted around in the water. Even when they want to move from place to place, they often hold on to a loose piece of plant life or debris to help weigh them down and give them more control as they ride the currents.

LIFE IN THE SLOW LANE

Seahorses have many skills, but they're firm failures in the swimming department. In fact, **dwarf seahorses** are the slowest fish in the entire world!

▶ A seahorse's odd, elongated body shape isn't built for speed, and the fact that they swim completely upright doesn't help.

▶ Seahorses don't have a lot in the way of fins. They have two small ones on the sides of their heads to help them steer and one slightly larger one on their back to propel them through the water . . . slowly!

▶ A seahorse can move its back fin from side to side an impressive 35 times every second, but even then it still only travels 5 feet per hour. That means if an average 12-year-old human were lying down, it would take a seahorse an entire hour to swim from their toes to the top of their head.

▶ Seahorses do have some things going for them—they have a body part called a "swim bladder" that can be pumped with varying amounts of air, helping them float at the right depth in the water.

WHAT DO SEAHORSES EAT?

Seahorses might be small, awkward swimmers, but that doesn't stop them from being voracious hunters!

▶ Seahorses don't have to chase down their prey; they wait for it to come to them. They latch on to a plant or piece of coral with their tails and wait, and then eat anything that drifts by.

▶ Seahorses suck up their prey through their snouts, which are great for reaching into small spaces. Depending on how much food they're trying to scoff down at once, their snouts can get bigger to fit it all in.

▶ They eat huge amounts of plankton and small crustaceans. Some species can eat a mammoth 3,000 brine shrimp in just one day!

▶ Seahorses don't have teeth or stomachs, so their food moves through them pretty quickly. It's hard to feel full when you don't have a stomach, which is why they're always eating!

HiDE-[AND]-SEEK

Seahorses are small, they don't have the ability to bite or sting, and they definitely can't outswim predators—so how do they stop themselves from becoming dinner for one of the many dangerous beasties dwelling in the ocean? It's a simple strategy—they hide!

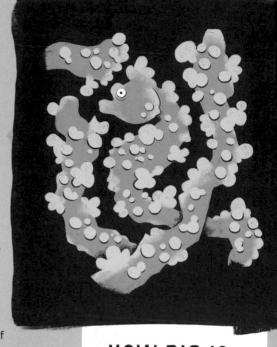

- ▶ Seahorses have special cells full of pigment near the surface of their skin, which help them quickly change color to match their surroundings when they're under threat.

- ▶ Not all color changes are caused by danger—they can also show how the seahorse is feeling. When it's dancing with its mate, the shifts in color are often elaborate.

- ▶ Some seahorses develop a permanent color to match their home. Some types of **pygmy seahorses** will turn purple or orange, depending on the color of the coral they live on. Two orange parents can end up with purple offspring if the fry drift off and land on purple coral.

- ▶ Seahorses can change the texture of their skin to blend in even more seamlessly with their environment. They can develop lumps, bumps, and rough patches to look more like coral, as well as algae and other plant life.

HOW BIG IS A HORSE?

Big-belly seahorses are the largest species. They grow up to 14 inches long, which is about half the length of a skateboard. As their name suggests, they have a particularly rotund tummy! The smallest seahorses are called "pygmies." One of the tiniest, the **Japan pig**, is about the same size as a grain of rice. They live near the coast of Japan and *apparently* look like baby pigs—that comparison might be a bit of a stretch, but you'd probably agree that they're as cute as piglets.

DEDiCATED DADS

Unlike just about every other animal, seahorse dads are the ones that get pregnant—at least in a sense. During mating, the female puts her eggs into the father's special brood pouch. He fertilizes them and then carries them around until they're ready to be born. After about 30 days the seahorse eggs turn into squiggly little seahorse fry, which shoot out of their father's pouch like streamers from a party popper. He can give birth to an astounding 2,000 fry in one go, and get pregnant again with the next lot the very same day.

CLIMATE CHANGE

Because they often live in such delicately balanced environments, the slightest changes to the climate can wreak havoc for seahorses. As climate change affects things like coral reefs and seagrass beds, seahorses are struggling, leading to 11 different types being classified as vulnerable or endangered.

FLANNERY FILE

You rarely see seahorses in the water, because they're so well disguised. When I went snorkeling as a kid, I sometimes saw them. But, more often, I would find them washed ashore after a winter storm. They seem to appear in the most surprising places—I often find them at my local beach. You have to look *so carefully* in the seaweed to spot them. When I do find one, it always feels exciting—no matter how many I've seen before. There are plenty of other things to find on the beach after a storm, too—paper nautiluses, pufferfish, and lots of good shells.

STRICTLY BALLROOM

Male and female seahorse pairs mate for life, and they can often be seen twining their tails together so they don't get separated. As if that's not cute enough, they also dance together every morning to build their attachment to each other. With their tails curled together they spin around, changing color as they sway gracefully through the waves.

BRAINY FISH

Seahorses have an odd connection with your brain. No, they're not telepathic—just brain-shaped. The part of your brain that deals with your memories is called the "hippocampus," which is also the scientific name for seahorses. This vital chunk of brain looks like an elongated, curved ridge with bumps along it—just like a seahorse.

EASY, TIGER

Seahorses make a growling sound when they're feeling upset.

CROCODILES

Crocodiles are often seen lazing about in the water or lumbering along slowly on land, but don't underestimate them! They're excellent at sneaking, hiding, and general lurking, but can also be incredibly fast and surprisingly athletic when they need to be. Most animals (and you should probably count yourself among them) can't think of anything worse than getting a close-up of a crocodile's mouth, but, for a special few, the inside of a crocodile's mouth isn't a bad place to be. Crocodiles might be fearsome hunters, but they also have a softer side!

WHERE CAN I SEE A CROCODILE?

They live in Australia, Asia, South and North America, and Africa.

WHEN THEY'RE ON LAND, A GROUP OF CROCODILES IS CALLED A BASK. IN THE WATER, THEY'RE CALLED A FLOAT.

WHO WOULD BABYSIT A CROCODILE?

CROCODILES CAN LIVE UP TO 75 YEARS.

SONG AND DANCE

▶ Crocodile mothers have to guard their eggs so that predators don't eat them. It's a big job, sometimes lasting more than three months, so some mothers hire help. **Nile crocodiles** have worked out a deal with nesting curlews—the birds help keep an eye on the eggs, and in return the mother crocodiles protect the bird babysitters from predators.

▶ When crocodile babies are ready to hatch they start to make sounds inside their eggs, telling siblings in neighboring eggs that it's time to break free. Their mother can also hear these tiny sounds, so she'll be ready to scoop up her babies and carry them to the water as soon as they hatch. How does a crocodile carry babies? Not in its tiny arms, that's for sure. They open up their mouths, let the babies clamber in and carry them there among all those sharp teeth!

Crocodiles wriggle around, slap the water, blow bubbles, and make bellowing sounds to attract a mate. Males can also release a stinky musk, a bit like how humans put on perfume or cologne, which you can see like an oily slick on the surface of the water.

GROSS!

WATER • CROCODILES

HOW BIG IS A CROCODILE?

Saltwater crocodiles are the biggest reptiles living on Earth today. The largest one ever found weighed over 2,370 pounds, about the same as two grand pianos, and was an astounding 20 feet, 3 inches long. That's over *three times* the height of LeBron James.

The smallest are the **dwarf crocodiles**, which can weigh as little as 40 pounds and are generally about 5 feet long. They're considered small for a crocodile, but if they stood on their tail they'd most likely still be taller than you!

The largest crocodile to ever live was probably the *Sarcosuchus imperator*, which was alive 110 million years ago, weighed 10 tons and was 36 feet long.

HOW DO YOU TELL THE DIFFERENCE BETWEEN A CROCODILE AND AN ALLIGATOR?

One easy way to tell the difference is by taking a look at their teeth—from a safe distance, of course! When an alligator's mouth is closed you can't see any of its teeth. Not crocodiles, though! They have two large teeth on their bottom jaw, one on either side, and they stick out even when their jaws are shut.

CROCODILE TOOTHBRUSHES

A crocodile with gaping jaws and small birds hopping around between its teeth is a very odd sight, but quite a common one. The birds are called plovers, and they don't have a death wish—they just know that the crocodile won't eat them because they do an excellent job of cleaning parasites from its gums!

SUPER SENSES

Crocodiles have lots of small bumps all over their bodies, with extra on their heads and near their teeth. These bumps are more sensitive than the tip of your finger—if they're swimming underwater, their bumps help them feel something as small as a raindrop hitting the water's surface.

KEEPING COOL

When crocodiles get too hot they open their jaws up really wide, a bit like how a dog pants to cool down. No matter how hot they get, crocodiles never sweat.

DISPOSABLE TEETH

Crocodiles lose and regrow teeth all the time—they go through about 8,000 teeth in a lifetime.

WHAT BIG TEETH YOU HAVE!

Crocodiles have very strong jaws—they can bite through bone with ease—but they're only strong when they're biting down on something. Crocodiles have barely any power to open their jaws, so all it takes to keep a crocodile from snapping is a piece of string tied around its jaws.

ON THE HUNT

Crocodiles are carnivorous, and they're also apex predators. So they're doubly dangerous! Some species go after smaller prey, including fish and birds, but the larger species need bigger meals—they eat things like monkeys, buffalo, hippos, and even sharks!

▶ Because their eyes and nostrils sit on top of their heads, crocodiles can stay almost completely submerged in water while still breathing and looking around. Crocs lurk like this near the edge of the water, lunging out to attack animals as they bend down to drink.

▶ **American** and **marsh crocodiles** sometimes lie under the water with sticks balanced on top of their heads. They only seem to do this during nesting season, when birds are particularly keen to gather sticks to build their nests. When the birds get close enough, lured by the sticks, the crocodiles surge out of the water and snap them up.

▶ Despite having heavy bodies and short legs, crocodiles can propel themselves out of the water with great speed—they use their long, powerful tails to launch.

▶ Crocodiles often do something called a "death roll" where they hold on to part of their prey's body and roll over multiple times to tear it off. They can do this both on land and in the water and will keep on rolling until their prey stops struggling—usually when it dies.

WILL A CROCODILE EAT YOU?

Yes, many types of crocodiles will attack and even eat humans. The saltwater species can be particularly dangerous, so if you're heading into their home territory make sure to take care where you swim.

FLANNERY FILE

When I was in my twenties I went on an expedition to Papua New Guinea. We walked for a couple of days to reach a remote village. I thought I'd take a shortcut back and inflated my airbed and floated down the river. It was a great day, circling gently in whirlpools and watching wildlife, including birds of prey such as kites circling overhead. But when I returned to our starting point a village man looked angrily at me. He took me to his house, which had the skull of an enormous crocodile on the wall, then pointed to the river I'd rafted down on my airbed. I'd been very silly indeed.

SHARKS

Sharks have a reputation for being fearsome hunters, which is very much deserved for certain species. Many sharks don't pose any threat to you, though—from the tiny sharks that don't have mouths big enough to bite your ankle to the gentle giants that only eat plankton. You'd also be surprised at some of the things that can hurt a shark. Spoiler alert: one of these things is the water they live in! Sharks do things that are endlessly fascinating, like eat their pesky siblings and live in volcanoes. Yes, that's really true.

WHERE CAN I SEE A SHARK?

Sharks live in every ocean on the planet, from freezing arctic waters to warm tropical beaches.

ANCIENT GIANTS

Megalodons are extinct sharks that lived between 2 million and 25 million years ago. They were 50 feet long and had jaws strong enough to crush a car— or a whale, which is what they hunted (cars didn't exist then).

WHALE SHARK PATTERNS

The patterns on whale sharks are highly varied, like human fingerprints—no two whale sharks have the same pattern.

DON'T POKE MY EYE!

Sharks are pretty tough, but they still have weak spots: their eyes. Some sharks have an extra eyelid, which is a thin but strong membrane that sits underneath their external eyelids and gives an extra layer of protection to their eyeballs. Not all sharks have this, so they have to find another way to keep their eyes safe from their flailing prey. The **great white shark** uses a pretty basic solution—it just rolls its eyes back so you can only see the whites of the eyes. One handy side effect is that it makes them look even more intimidating!

HUNTING AND EATING

Most sharks are carnivores. Common shark snacks include fish, sea lions, seals, dolphins, turtles, rays, and plankton, but hungry sharks have been known to eat all sorts of things. The skull of a polar bear was once found in the stomach of a **Greenland shark**!

▶ **Whale sharks** take in a huge amount of water as they gulp down mouthfuls of plankton and tiny fish. They can't drink it all, so they filter in the food and spit the unwanted water back out. They can expel up to 400,000 gallons of water per hour, which gives you an idea of how much these giant sharks eat.

▶ For some sharks, the smell of blood in the water is enough to send them into a feeding frenzy. A **great white shark** can sense just one drop of blood in 26 gallons of sea water.

▶ **Thresher sharks** are so flexible they can bend their bodies in half. Their tails can be as long as their entire body, and they use them to hunt by flipping them forward so violently that the fish they hit are smashed into pieces!

▶ **Cookie-cutter sharks** are only about 1 foot long, but they have huge, triangular teeth in their lower jaws. They feed by swimming up to whales and other large marine mammals and biting, then twisting, to cut out a circle of flesh. Whales are sometimes covered with the circular scars left by these sharks.

A GROUP OF SHARKS IS CALLED A SHIVER.

LONG LIVES

Greenland sharks can often live for 272 years, and possibly even up to 400 years. That's longer than any other vertebrate on Earth! These sharks keep growing as adults, but only grow a third of an inch each year.

Knowing how old a shark is can be tricky, and there is plenty of room for error. The most common method is by counting the rings of cartilage that build up over time on their spines. This is similar to the way trees can be aged by counting the rings within their trunks. You can tell how old Greenland sharks are by counting the layers on their eyeballs, which grow new layers over time.

PESKY PARASITES

Ninety percent of **Greenland sharks** have a parasite that lives and feeds on their eyeballs. These parasites cause so much damage that the sharks become blind. Luckily they spend most of their time deep in cold, dark waters, so they're not dependent on eyesight.

CAN SHARKS DROWN?

Some sharks need to swim constantly so that they can breathe. Sharks don't actually breathe through their nostrils; they only use those for smelling. They use their gills to breathe—pulling fresh water in through their mouths as they swim, absorbing the oxygen, then passing the water out through their gills. If they stop swimming, their access to fresh supplies of oxygen-filled water also stops. Some types of shark do have a nifty way around this—instead of waiting for water to flow through their mouths and gills, they actively suck water in and force it out through their gills, which means they can stop swimming and still access oxygen-rich water.

SHARKCANO

It sounds too wild to be true, but a group of scientists have discovered sharks living inside an underwater volcano! It's not a dormant volcano, either. The volcano's name is Kavachi and it sits underneath the surface of the Pacific Ocean. The water around it is hot, acidic, and cloudy, which makes it hard for lots of marine creatures to live there, so scientists are still looking into how the sharks are able to survive. Researching this incredible discovery is tricky, because sending a human into such a volatile area isn't wise. But the scientists have found an incredibly cool way to gather the information they need—they're sending in robots!

AMAZING!

One of my favorite sharks is the **wobbegong**. It can grow up to 10 feet long, and has strange, seaweed-like protrusions around its mouth. It spends most of its time on the sea bottom, or in sea caves. When I used to scuba-dive off the coast of Victoria I often found them lurking, sometimes covered in small crayfish, in submarine caves. They were very docile. But you must never touch their tails, because they can turn around with lightning speed and bite you if you do! I've swum with sharks a number of times, and, to me, sharks are really very similar to dogs. They're friendly and inquisitive creatures; you've just got to be a bit cautious, like you would be with a big dog. Having to share a space with sharks teaches you a new respect for nature. In the Pacific Islands, people swim with sharks and crocodiles all the time, because they know their movements and habits. Likewise, the crocodiles and sharks know people's movements and habits. Some of the sharks and the crocodiles are probably as old as the people who are swimming!

BEACH BATHING

We often think of sharks hanging around beaches, but although some sharks do like to be near coastlines, plenty of sharks prefer the open ocean or even the deep sea where there is no sunlight. **Basking sharks** spend most of their time deep underwater, where humans can't see them, and only about 10 percent of their time near the ocean's surface. Some sharks, such as the **bull shark**, can live in fresh water as well as salt water, swimming inland through rivers.

HOW BIG ARE SHARKS?

The **whale shark** is the largest fish in the world. They can grow to 40 feet long and weigh up to 28 tons, more than four African elephants. At the opposite end of the spectrum, the **dwarf lantern shark** can be as small as 6 inches long.

KEEPING THE TOOTH FAIRY BUSY

Sharks have an astounding number of teeth that grow in multiple rows in their mouths. **Great whites** have up to 300 teeth and some sharks have even more! Sharks regularly lose their teeth (one of the hazards of being so keen on biting things), so they need to have plenty of teeth ready to replace the ones that fall out. When they lose a tooth, one from the row behind moves forward to fill the space, kind of like a conveyor belt filled with teeth.

FAST MOVERS

Shortfin makos can swim up to 60 miles per hour and are the fastest sharks in the world, followed by **salmon sharks** and **great whites**.

A SHARK CAN GO THROUGH 50,000 TEETH OVER ITS LIFETIME.

WHAT DOES ELECTRICITY HAVE TO DO WITH SHARKS?

Sharks have something called "electroreception," which is pretty much a superpower. They have a whole lot of pores on their snouts that are filled with a special kind of jelly that is very sensitive to electric energy. This jelly allows sharks to sense tiny electric currents caused by fish and other marine animals moving in the water. The jelly can even pick up on a movement as tiny as the heartbeat of a fish, allowing sharks to home in on their prey with ease. **NEAT!**

CLIMATE CHANGE

As oceans warm with climate change, some sharks are spreading out to follow their food sources. Other sharks that used to migrate with the seasons to reach warmer waters are staying put, because their home is now warm enough year-round.

As an apex predator, sharks are vital for keeping delicate marine ecosystems in balance.

OLDER THAN DINOSAURS

There are more than 450 different species of shark swimming in oceans all around the world, and many of them are relatives of ancient creatures.

▶ The **sixgill shark** has ancestors that lived 20 million years before dinosaurs.

▶ The **frilled shark** has been around for about 80 million years and hasn't changed much in that time. The modern frilled shark has a long, snake-like body and a hinged jaw packed with 300 thin, super-sharp teeth.

SINGLE PARENTS AND SIBLING RIVALRY

Some female sharks, like **bonnethead** and **leopard sharks**, can give birth without ever meeting a male! This usually only happens when there are no males around, and babies born in this way are always female.

Sand tiger sharks have two wombs. Why? Because these brutal babies eat their weaker siblings in the womb! If these sharks didn't have two wombs to keep their murderous offspring separate, they'd only ever have one baby at a time. It's survival of the hungriest!

PLATYPUSES

WHERE CAN I SEE A PLATYPUS?

Platypuses live in the eastern and southeastern parts of Australia.

When platypuses were first discovered, some scientists thought someone had stitched together the body parts of different animals—like a swimming version of Frankenstein's monster—just to trick them! That's because platypuses look like a strange mix of a duck, a beaver, and an otter. Their scientific name, **Ornithorhynchus anatinus**, even means "bird-snout duck-like." Platypuses don't just *look* weird, they also act weird—the way their babies are born (and fed!) is particularly odd—and they're not quite as cuddly as they seem, either.

CLIMATE CHANGE

Climate change could affect platypuses by reducing rainfall and increasing evaporation. This could dry up the streams and rivers that they depend upon.

PLATYPUSES ARE RARELY FOUND IN GROUPS, BUT A GROUP OF THEM WOULD BE CALLED A PADDLE.

UNDERWATER **BUFFET**

Platypuses live in riverbank burrows, and although they can walk on land they spend most of their time swimming and hunting in the water. They generally go for small prey like insect larvae, tadpoles, shrimp, and the kinds of beetles and bugs that swim. If an unsuspecting flying insect lands on the surface of the water it could also become a tasty snack!

▸ Platypuses hunt for an astounding 10 to 12 hours every day.

▸ They can eat their body weight in food over the space of 24 hours.

▸ Platypuses can't see, hear or smell underwater, but their remarkable bills are able to pick up on tiny electric currents caused by their prey moving through the water. You could say their bills are their secret weapons!

▸ Platypuses can stay underwater for 30 to 140 seconds. When they're looking for food, they make lots of quick dives, scooping insects, gravel, and leaf litter from the riverbed and filtering through it for things to eat. They store whatever food they find in special cheek pouches until they come back up to the surface, where they float as they eat.

TURTLE CRUNCHERS

Scientists have found a fossilized tooth from an ancient type of platypus called *Obdurodon tharalkooschild* (what a mouthful!), which lived between 5 million and 15 million years ago. These creatures are thought to have grown to about 3 feet long and weigh four times as much as the platypuses living today. They also had heaps of powerful teeth that might have been strong enough to crunch up baby turtles!

BUILT TO SWIM

Platypuses have bodies that are decidedly ungraceful on land, but in the water it's a whole different story.

▸ Their thick fur is waterproof, keeping them cozy as they swim.

▸ Their feet have webbing between the toes, making them perfect for paddling and steering through the water. It's kind of unhelpful to have webbing when you're trying to dig a burrow, though, so they have the ability to retract the webbing to give their claws all the room they need to dig!

▸ When platypuses dive, they close their eyes and ears with special flaps of skin. They even have a built-in nose seal that stops water from filling their nostrils when they dive. Handy!

▸ Platypuses are SPEEDY under the water. The bodies that waddle on land are suddenly capable of zipping along at 3 feet per second.

MILK FED

When platypus babies hatch, they're only slightly larger than a jelly bean. Their mothers feed them milk, but not in the usual way. The milk oozes out of pores in the mother's belly instead—kind of like how sweat appears on your skin after a bike ride. A platypus baby has to lick the milk right off its mother's stomach!

Wow!

FLANNERY FILE

I got to help name the fossilized remains of the oldest ancestor of a platypus ever discovered. The fossil was one of the weirdest I've ever seen—it was a jaw with teeth that had all turned into opal! It was very beautiful, with colorful flashes and parts so clear that you could see right through them! We named it *Steropodon*, which means "lightning tooth," because it had been found at a place called Lightning Ridge in New South Wales.

POISONOUS COWBOYS

Platypuses are one of the only venomous mammals in the world! Males have special venom glands that are connected to sharp, half-inch-long spurs near their back feet, kind of like the spurs on cowboy boots. The venom that comes out of the spurs is powerful enough to kill a dog, but luckily isn't lethal to humans. It is very painful, though!

HOW BIG ARE THEY?

Platypuses are usually between 15 and 23 inches long, about the size of a small dog.

CONGRATULATIONS ON THE BIRTH OF YOUR . . . EGG

Most mammals, including humans, give birth to fully formed babies. But not the platypus! They're one of only two mammals in the entire world that lay eggs (the other is the echidna). Platypus mothers don't sit on their eggs to keep them warm in the burrow—they cradle the eggs against their stomachs and fold up their wide tails to hold them in place.

MISSING BODY PARTS

- Carnivores need teeth, right? Wrong! Platypuses don't have any, just flat plates to grind their food against. They use the bits of rock scooped up along with their food as temporary teeth to help mash the food inside their bills. Weirdly, platypus babies actually have small teeth when they're first born, but they fall out pretty quickly.

- Platypuses don't have a stomach. Their gullets connect straight to their intestines, meaning their mouths and butts are one step closer than they are in your body. A stomach is generally pretty vital for breaking down food, but platypuses eat things that can be digested without the help of one.

• FLANNERY FILE •

Platypuses are super-secretive animals. They spend most of the day snoozing in their riverbank burrows, and when they leave their hidey-holes they usually dive straight into the water, so they can be hard to spot. When I was a teenager I was walking along a creek in western Victoria. It was early in the morning, and I had no idea that there were platypuses living in the creek, which flowed through farmland. I reached a small bluff and there, just below me, was a platypus, resting on top of the water. Luckily it didn't see me, so I stood still for around 15 minutes and watched as it dived, swam, and fed in the clear water. It was one of the most magical experiences of my life.

TURTLES AND TORTOISES

Turtles and tortoises are both types of Testudines (say that tongue twister three times fast!). "Testudines" means "shell," and you can't miss that feature on these creatures—their shells cover most of their bodies. So how do you tell the difference between turtles and tortoises? It all comes down to where they live—turtles can spend time on land, but they generally prefer the water. Some live in the ocean, others prefer fresh water. Tortoises always live on land.

Turtles and tortoises have been around since the dinosaurs, so they've had plenty of time to develop some weird habits, including breathing through their butts, imitating worms, and growing green mohawks.

WHERE CAN I SEE A TURTLE OR TORTOISE?

There are turtles or tortoises on every continent except Antarctica.

54

HOW DO TURTLES BREATHE?

Some turtles come to the water's surface regularly to breathe, but certain freshwater turtles hibernate all winter underwater, and others barely come up for air year-round. So, how do they do it?

- The **mata mata turtle** uses its bizarrely long snout like you would use a snorkel.

- The **common musk turtle** has a special tongue that is covered in little buds that draw oxygen out of the water, so it breathes through its tongue as it swims.

- The Australian **Fitzroy River turtle** absorbs oxygen through its cloaca, or, in simple terms, it breathes through its butt. Yes, seriously. **CLEVER!**

STINK ATTACK

Musk turtles, also called stinkpot turtles, are small enough to sit in your hand. When they feel threatened, they release an overpoweringly bad smell from musk glands underneath their shells. It smells so bad that most predators will back off.

FREE WORMS →

WHAT'S FOR DINNER?

Tortoises eat plants, and some turtles are partial to plant-based snacks as well, but for the most part turtles are carnivorous—and they've come up with some pretty ingenious ways to catch their meals.

- The **alligator snapping turtle** lives in rivers and lakes in the United States. It has a sneaky way of hunting that involves poking out its long, pink tongue and wiggling it around so it looks like a worm. Passing creatures that are lured in to try to eat the "worm" get snapped up in the turtle's powerful, beak-like jaws.

- **Leatherback turtles** have a whole lot of spiny barbs inside their throats that help them eat jellyfish. The barbs point toward their stomach so it's easy for jellies to slide down, but if they try to slither back out they get spiked! These turtles can eat more than 220 pounds of jellyfish each day, so they play an important part in controlling jellyfish populations.

- **Cantor's giant softshell turtles** bury themselves in the mud in the water, leaving just their eyes and mouths poking out. They only go to the surface to breathe twice a day! They stay completely still, and then when a fish or crab wanders past they snap it up with lightning speed. Their dinner never sees them coming.

- **Wood turtles** love eating worms, and they've developed a clever way to catch them. The turtles stomp their feet to imitate the sound of raindrops hitting the ground, luring earthworms out into the open where they can be gobbled up by the waiting turtle.

FLANNERY FILE

Mary River turtles are often called by a much more unusual name—the green-haired punk turtle! They get their name from their super-weird hairstyles—they sport tufts of bright green hair that often look like mohawks. Here's the twist, though—the "hair" is actually a type of algae. These turtles also have two fleshy spikes sticking out from under their jaws, which look like a strange beard or even two pointy teeth. I once saw a Mary River turtle in the wild, with its long, green "hair." What really amazed me was how big it was! Its tail alone was as thick as my arm. Mary River turtles are butt-breathing turtles—they breathe through their cloacae—hence their massive tails. These amazing animals have probably lived in the Mary River in Australia for millions of years. They used to be in many other river systems as well, but they have only survived in one. I felt like I was in the presence of reptilian nobility!

A GROUP OF TURTLES iS CALLED A BALE (OR A NEST), WHiLE A GROUP OF TORTOiSES iS SOMETiMES REFERRED TO AS A CREEP.

A PORTABLE HOME

Unlike hermit crabs, turtles and tortoises don't outgrow their shells. They never have to go looking for a new, bigger shell, because their shell is part of their skeleton—it's just outside of their body instead of inside, like ours. Some turtles and tortoises can pull their heads and feet inside their shells for protection, but not all of them are that lucky—some are stuck with permanently exposed limbs.

CLIMATE CHANGE

The sex of baby sea turtles is decided in the egg by the temperature of the sand they are laid in. Typically, males hatch from eggs that are kept at less than 80 degrees Fahrenheit, and females hatch from eggs that sit in temperatures higher than 86. With climate change warming our planet, scientists are finding that the number of female sea turtles is jumping way beyond the number of males, which will make it trickier for them to mate in the future.

꞊ TEENY TiNY ꞊
OR UNBELIEVABLY BIG

South Africa's **speckled Cape tortoise** is the smallest type of Testudines. They can weigh as little as 3.5 ounces and their shells are only 2 to 4 inches long! That means the smallest of these miniature tortoises can be held in the palm of your hand.

The biggest type of Testudines is the **leatherback turtle**, which lives in salt water and can weigh a whopping 2,000 pounds. That's the same weight as 150 bowling balls, and if you've ever been bowling, you'll know how heavy just one of those is.

BORN ON THE BEACH

All female turtles need to come onto land to lay their eggs, and sea turtles like to return to the exact same beach they were born on to lay their eggs. They usually haven't seen that particular beach since they were a coin-sized hatchling (which might have been decades ago) so nobody knows how they manage to find their way back! Sometimes they travel thousands of miles to lay their eggs. When they get there, female sea turtles dig a deep pit in the sand with their flippers and lay up to 200 eggs before filling it up with sand and swimming back into the ocean. After two months the eggs hatch, and the tiny baby turtles need to dig their way out of the sand and race down the beach into the water. If they're not quick, animals such as crabs, lizards, and birds scoop them up and eat them!

A TURTLE IN A TREE?

Even though turtles can walk around on land you probably wouldn't expect to see one in a tree. But **big-headed turtles** aren't your average turtle—they've been seen using their big beaky jaws and long tails to clamber up into bushes and trees! As you can guess by the name, these turtles have a comically large head that is about half the size of their entire shell, complete with huge jaws.

OCTOPUSES

You can tell just by looking at them that octopuses are weird. They're smart, secretive and really good at avoiding trouble— sometimes by pretending to be a lump of coral, other times by shooting ink everywhere like an exploding pen. Their bulbous, brainy bodies can squeeze into tiny spaces, because they're almost completely boneless, and sometimes they even break off one of their arms—you'll never guess why!

WHERE CAN I SEE AN OCTOPUS?

Octopuses live in oceans all around the world. Many prefer shallow waters in slightly warmer areas, but some live in deep, dark, and very cold parts of the sea.

A GROUP OF OCTOPUSES iS SOMETiMES CALLED A CONSORTiUM, BUT THEY VERY RARELY HANG OUT iN GROUPS—THEY PREFER TO BE ALONE.

ON THE HUNT

Octopuses are carnivores, usually targeting smaller marine animals such as crabs, shrimp, lobster, and fish.

▶ Many octopuses, including the **pale octopus**, use their powerful arms to pull apart shellfish and eat the flesh inside. They can even pull open oysters! Their beaks are powerful too. They're shaped like a parrot's beak and can crack into shells.

▶ If it comes across a shell that is too tough to pull open or crack, the **common octopus** has a toothed tongue that it uses to drill into shells. It has toxic saliva that it can inject into the holes to disarm the animal inside and make it easier to pry open the shell.

▶ Sharks can sometimes fall prey to hungry octopuses. They use their many arms to hold the sharks tight and their surprisingly sharp, beaky mouths to tear into their flesh.

▶ Octopuses often drop down onto their prey from above, using the suckers on their arms to latch on to their prey and force them into their mouths.

▶ If *you* want to taste something you need to put it in your mouth, but octopuses can taste with every part of their skin. Imagine being able to squish some ice-cream onto your elbow and immediately be able to tell if it was strawberry or chocolate flavored! The suckers on octopuses' arms are extra sensitive, with about 200 tastebuds packed onto each arm.

EATING JELLY

Some types of octopus are immune to jellyfish venom, so they can safely make a meal out of them. It's one thing to gobble down a jelly, but multiple types of octopus have also been seen toting around venomous Portuguese man-of-war and fried egg jellies after catching and killing them. The reason is really clever—they're using the trailing stingers of the jellies to catch food, as well as to protect themselves.

LADIES AND GENTLEMEN

Male and female octopuses are often startlingly different sizes. Female **blanket octopuses** are about 6 feet wide, but males are a mere 1 inch! The females of this species are also 40,000 times heavier than the males and have huge sheets of red, patterned skin between their arms. As they swim, they can unfurl these sheets of skin and trail them like a billowing cloak.

MIRACULOUS BODIES

- Octopuses don't just have one heart—they have three! One pumps blood around the body and the other two pump blood to the gills. The heart that supplies blood to the body stops beating when they're swimming, which is one of the reasons octopuses prefer to walk when they can.

- Human blood is iron-based, which makes it red. Octopus blood is copper-based, which makes it blue. The copper in their blood helps carry oxygen around their bodies at very low temperatures, so the octopuses that live in the freezing water around Antarctica have extra copper in their blood. That means their blood is extra blue!

- Octopuses can release a black, inky substance into the water when they're scared. The ink, which is partly made of mucus, makes it harder for predators to smell, taste, and see. The ink is so powerful that it can hurt the octopus, too, so the octopus needs to make a speedy getaway while its enemy is busy being blinded with black snot.

- If an octopus loses an arm—maybe in a fight, or escaping a predator—it can regrow the missing limb. **HANDY!**

THROWING A *TANTRUM* ARGH

Some octopuses living on the Australian coastline have been seen picking up shells and throwing them at each other. That's taking antisocial behavior to a whole new level!

HAPPY FAMILIES

The decision to start a family is a risky business for octopuses.

- Male octopuses have eight arms, just like females, but one of their arms is pretty unusual—it's full of sperm. Female octopuses often kill and eat males after mating, so some males have come up with a clever way to avoid becoming dinner. They snap off their special baby-making arm, give it to their mate and make a quick escape. Drastic!

- Female octopuses lay tens of thousands of eggs—sometimes more than 100,000 in one go. The mother protects them from predators, keeps them clean, and makes sure they're getting enough oxygen until they hatch, which sometimes takes months. The mother regularly goes without food over this time and will actually eat her own arms before she'll leave her eggs to find food!

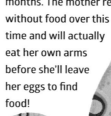
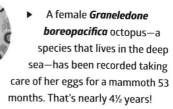

- A female ***Graneledone boreopacifica*** octopus—a species that lives in the deep sea—has been recorded taking care of her eggs for a mammoth 53 months. That's nearly 4½ years!

ON THE ROAD AGAIN...

WITH A
MOBILE HOME

Coconut octopuses carry a portable house around with them, like humans use camper vans. These clever critters find two halves of a shell and tuck them underneath their bodies, using a few arms to hold them in place as they waddle along. It's not graceful, but it does mean that if they come across anything frightening they can climb inside one shell half and use their suckers to slam the other half shut on top of themselves.

MASTERS OF DISGUISE

With their bizarrely shaped bodies you'd think octopuses would stand out, but they can be amazingly hard to spot.

▶ Octopuses have thousands of cells on the surface of their skin that are filled with different colors. By expanding or tightening their skin they can choose which colors are visible, letting them change to match whatever they're near. They can even create stripes or spots of color.

▶ As long as their bony beak can fit, octopuses can twist and contort the rest of their boneless bodies to squeeze into tiny gaps and cracks.

▶ By contracting special muscles across their bodies octopuses can change the texture of their skin from smooth to rough, spiky, or wispy, depending on what kind of rock, sand, seaweed or coral they need to blend into.

▶ Some octopuses bury themselves in the sand to hide—the **hammer octopus** stays buried all day and only emerges at night to hunt.

▶ One type of octopus is so good at disguises that it has been given the name **mimicking miracle octopus.** These tricksters can mold their bodies to look like a whole host of different animals, including sea snakes, eels, and lionfish. If there is a predator approaching the octopus can either imitate an animal that looks dull and inedible so it doesn't get eaten, or mimic an animal that the predator is afraid of so that it hightails it out of there.

GENIUS!

ON THE RUN

Octopuses have been known to climb out of the water for short periods of time when it suits them, but why would an octopus ever want to be out of the water? In the wild, they might make a quick foray out onto a rock to catch a crab or some other snack. In captivity, the stakes are much higher! In New Zealand, an enterprising octopus named Inky staged a miraculous escape by climbing out of his tank, walking through the aquarium, squeezing into a narrow pipe, and slithering down into the sea.

The ancient Romans recorded octopuses climbing out of the sea at night to raid the factories where the famous fish sauce garum was made.

CLIMATE CHANGE

The blue blood that octopuses have is sensitive to acid levels in the water. Too much acid makes it hard for their blood to keep moving oxygen around the body. As oceans become more acidic with climate change, they'll find it harder to get enough oxygen.

GET OUT OF MY ROOM!

Octopuses are secretive creatures that spend a lot of time skulking in caves and rock crevices. Their hidey-hole is called a "den," and if they can't find one that suits them they'll build their own. They pick up rocks and stack them to make walls, and even make rock doors that they can pull shut. Octopuses also decorate the area around their dens with the shells of snails and clams they've eaten—making an octopus's garden.

TAKING YOUR
BREATH AWAY

Blue-ringed octopuses are small, incredibly dangerous octopuses that live in coastal waters around Australia. They're quite common on rocky beaches, even near big cities, but they're shy and hard to spot. When they're scared, their brown skin flashes with electric blue rings, warning predators to back off. Their powerful venom can easily kill a human, but they're really shy and won't attack unless threatened. The stinging part of their body is so small that you don't always feel it when you're stung, but it's hard to miss the symptoms caused by their poisonous saliva—you'll have difficulty breathing, your lips and tongue will go numb, and your breathing muscles will eventually be completely paralyzed.

SCARY!

ANCIENT OCTOPUSES

The oldest octopus fossil that has been found belonged to a creature called *Pohlsepia*, which lived 296 million years ago, millions of years before the dinosaurs.

BUSES AND BEANS

The biggest octopus in the world is the **giant Pacific octopus**. The largest one ever found was more than 30 feet wide, which is a little longer than one of the original red double-decker buses from London, and weighed more than 600 pounds. The smallest is ***Octopus wolfi***, which is often shorter than 1 inch. These tiny creatures weigh less than a single jelly bean!

BRAINS IN THEIR ARMS?

Neurons are nerve cells that let us know what's going on in different parts of our bodies. For example, when you touch something hot, your neurons are what make you pull your hand away. For humans, a lot of our neurons are in our brains. Octopuses have neurons, too—like all animals—but instead of being mostly in their brains, 65 percent of them are in their arms! That means their arms are really good at doing lots of different things at once. You might find it hard doing two different things at once with your hands, like patting your head and rubbing your tummy, but an octopus can use each of its eight arms to do eight different things at once. They're multitasking champions!

SQUEE!

GLOSSARY

G
L
O
S
S
A
R
Y

ALGAE

Algae are a large and wide-ranging group of organisms, most of which are aquatic. Some are microscopic, while others (like many types of seaweed) can grow to be very large. They can be found in both salt water and fresh water.

ALPHA MALE/FEMALE

The alpha is the most powerful individual in a group of animals— the leader. There can be alpha males or alpha females, and some groups of animals are led by a pair of alphas—both male and female. Alphas usually gain leadership by fighting and defeating the former alpha.

AMPHIBIAN

Amphibians are small vertebrates that live in a wet environment. Amphibians include frogs, salamanders, and newts.

APEX PREDATOR

Apex predators are also called alpha predators or top predators. They are on the top of the food chain, which means that they have no natural predators to fear. They play an important role in maintaining a balanced and healthy ecosystem.

AQUATIC

Aquatic animals are those that spend all or most of their time in the water.

ATMOSPHERE

Atmosphere is the gases surrounding a planet, held there by the planet's gravity. Earth's atmosphere is a very thin layer of air between the earth's surface and the edge of space.

BACTERIA

Bacteria are microscopic single-celled organisms. They can be found in many different places: in the soil, air, and water, as well as on and inside plants and animals— including humans. Some bacteria are beneficial to us, whereas others are destructive.

BIOLUMINESCENCE

Bioluminescence is the production of light by a living organism. This glowing light is created by chemical reactions inside animals' bodies, and can be helpful in many different ways, from scaring off predators to finding food or a mate.

BLOOD CELLS

Blood is made up of blood cells, plus a liquid element called plasma. There are three kinds of blood cells: 1. red blood cells absorb oxygen from the lungs and transport it around the body, 2. white blood cells fight against disease and infection, 3. platelets help to clot the blood and heal wounds.

CANNIBALISM

Cannibalism is the act of eating a member of the same species. More than 1,500 species are known to do this. Some species will only turn to cannibalism when other foods are scarce, but for others, scarcity has little or nothing to do with the practice of eating each other.

CARBON

Carbon is a chemical element. It is one of the building blocks that plants and animals are made from, making it essential to all life on Earth. All organic compounds are considered "carbon-based." Carbon can combine with other elements to make new compounds.

CARBON DIOXIDE

Carbon dioxide is a compound made up of one carbon atom (C) and two oxygen atoms (O_2). It is a greenhouse gas, which means it traps the sun's heat close to the earth instead of allowing it to move out into space. Too much carbon dioxide causes the earth to overheat and, as the weather changes, many plants and animals are negatively affected. This is called global warming, or climate change.

CARBON EMISSIONS

When we burn carbon-rich fossil fuels, we release a huge amount of carbon into the air. The carbon then bonds with oxygen to produce carbon dioxide. Over time, the amount of carbon in the atmosphere has risen drastically due to the increased use of fossil fuels.

CARNIVORE/CARNIVOROUS

Carnivores are animals that exclusively or primarily eat meat—either by killing their meal or by scavenging carcasses.

CETACEANS

Cetaceans are a group of aquatic mammals that includes whales, porpoises, and dolphins. Many of them live in salt water.

COLD-BLOODED AND WARM-BLOODED ANIMALS

Warm-blooded animals, or endotherms, use their metabolism to generate the right amount of heat to keep their bodies at the right temperature. Cold-blooded animals, or ectotherms, aren't able to control their body temperature using their metabolism. On cold days, their metabolism drops along with their body temperature, which slows down their physical movement.

Endotherms generally need a steady food supply to keep their metabolism generating heat, while ectotherms can often survive long periods without food, thanks to their ability to slow their bodies down and wait out the colder months.

CONTINENTS

A continent is a large landmass, and one continent often includes multiple countries. The continents of the world are Europe, Asia, Africa, North and South America, Australia, and Antarctica.

CRUSTACEANS

Crustaceans are a diverse group of invertebrate animals. All crustaceans originally came from the sea, but some (such as slaters) have adapted to terrestrial life. All crustaceans have antennae and a tough exoskeleton. Crustaceans include such animals as shrimp, crabs, lobsters, crayfish, and krill.

CURRENTS

Ocean currents are sections of water that constantly flow in a particular direction. Some currents run along the surface of the water, while others run through the ocean's depths. Currents are affected by the wind, the earth's rotation, the temperature, differences in salinity (salt content of the water) and the gravitational pull of the moon.

DOMESTICATED SPECIES

Domesticated species are animals that have been bred to benefit humans, often over many generations. Animals are often domesticated so that humans can use parts of their bodies (such as flesh, skin, fur, or bone), or things that they produce (such as milk or eggs), for food, clothing, and decoration. Animals are also often domesticated to use as labor or to keep as pets.

DROUGHT

Drought is a prolonged period with much less rainfall than usual, or no rainfall at all. Drought causes rivers and lakes to dry up, which leaves many animals without water to drink. It causes plants to die, which can result in habitat loss and less food for animals to eat. Many animal populations are threatened by drought, and climate change is increasing the instances of drought around the world.

ECHOLOCATION

Echolocation is the use of echoes and soundwaves to find out where an object is in space. Many animals use echolocation to hunt and navigate, like dolphins, whales, bats, and some bird species.

ECOSYSTEM

An ecosystem is a finely balanced environment, in which all the living things (plants, animals and other organisms) and nonliving things (like rocks and the weather) work together to maintain the system's health.

EXOSKELETON

An exoskeleton is the hard, shell-like covering around some animals that functions to support and protect their body. All insects and crustaceans have exoskeletons; their skeleton is on the outside of their body. Some animals, such as turtles and tortoises, have both an exoskeleton (their shell) and an endoskeleton (the bones inside their bodies).

FERAL ANIMALS

Feral animals are domesticated animals that have been released into the wild and continued to reproduce there—for example, feral cats, goats, camels, and dogs. Feral animals can often endanger the lives of wild animals by preying on them.

FORAGING

When an animal searches for food in the wild, this is called foraging.

FOSSIL FUELS

Fossil fuels are made from fossilized plants and animals that have been buried under the soil for millions of years. Fossil fuels include things like oil, coal, and natural gas.

GREENHOUSE GAS EMISSIONS

Greenhouse gases absorb the heat that radiates off the earth's surface and bounce it back, trapping heat in the atmosphere rather than releasing it into space. The main greenhouse gases are water vapor, carbon dioxide, methane, and nitrous oxide. Fossil fuels are the biggest human cause of greenhouse gas emissions.

HERBIVORE/ HERBIVOROUS

Herbivores are animals that have an exclusively or primarily plant-based diet.

HIBERNATION

Hibernation is a type of deep rest that some endotherms, or warm-blooded animals, go into. Hibernation often occurs when animals don't have access to enough food or when it's too cold—certain species of animal hibernate over winter every year. During hibernation, body temperatures drop and metabolisms slow down as animals become inactive.

HIERARCHY

Hierarchy refers to a power structure within a group of animals. An alpha or an alpha pair is generally at the top of the hierarchy, with other members of the group having varying degrees of power below them. Omegas are the least powerful members of the hierarchy.

HORMONES

Hormones are chemicals inside plants and animals that help all of these living things to function. In plants, hormones help to control growth, as well as the production of flowers or fruit. In animals, hormones are used to send messages to different parts of the body to help it operate. Hormones affect all sorts of things, like growth, sleep, temperature, hunger, and much more.

HUNTING

For animals, hunting is the activity of killing and eating other animals. For humans, hunting also includes killing animals, but not always for food.

INCUBATION

Incubation is the process of keeping eggs at the right temperature while embryos grow inside them. Different animals incubate their eggs in different ways, such as sitting on them or burying them in sand, dirt, or plant matter.

INVERTEBRATE

Invertebrates lack a backbone; they either have a gooey, spongy body (like jellyfish and worms) or they have an exoskeleton (like insects and crabs).

KERATIN

Keratin is a strong, fibrous protein. It is the main substance that forms body parts like hair, nails, hoofs, horns, feathers, and the outermost layers of skin and scales.

KRILL

Krill are tiny swimming crustaceans. They eat phytoplankton, a microscopic type of plankton that generally grows near the ocean's surface. Krill are the main food source for hundreds of different animals, including fish, whales, and birds.

LARVAE

Many animals begin their life as larvae before eventually growing into their adult form. Larvae generally look completely different from their parents, and often need very different conditions to survive. For example, tadpoles are the larvae of frogs, and caterpillars are the larvae of butterflies.

MAMMALS

Mammals are a very broad class of animals. Some walk, some swim, and some fly, and their diets can vary from carnivorous to herbivorous, but they all have a number of traits in common, including that they have hair or fur, feed their young with milk, and are warm-blooded.

MARSUPIALS

Marsupials are a group of mammals. Most female marsupials have a pouch where they keep their babies when they're very young, so that they can continue to grow and develop in a safe, warm place. Some marsupial species are herbivores, others are carnivores, and there are also some omnivorous species. Most of the world's marsupials live in Australia and South America.

MEGAFAUNA

The word "megafauna" means "giant animal." It is most commonly used to refer to animals from the Pleistocene epoch (the end of the last ice age), which are the larger ancestors of animals alive today. However, species that are alive today can also be referred to as megafauna —common examples include elephants, rhinos, hippos, giraffes, lions, bears, and whales.

MEMBRANES

A membrane is a thin layer of tissue. Membranes can be found inside all living things—each cell inside a plant or animal is surrounded by a membrane—but membranes can also be found in many other places. Some animals are born completely surrounded by a membrane, which they then break out of, and other animals have protective membranes underneath their eyelids that help keep their eyes safe.

METABOLISM

Metabolism refers to the chemical reactions that happen inside an organism to keep it alive. There are many different metabolic reactions, but the main ones involve releasing energy or using energy. For example, an animal's metabolism digests the food it eats and converts that food into a form that can be released as energy. Animals also use their energy to grow and repair their bodies.

MIGRATION

Migration is a movement from one place to another. Animals often migrate each year at about the same time, and different species migrate for different reasons. Migrations commonly occur as animals travel to places where food is more plentiful, or the weather is better, or to places where they can find a mate or breed.

NOCTURNAL

Nocturnal animals are active during the night and rest during the day.

OMNIVORE/OMNIVOROUS

Omnivores are animals that eat a variety of meat and plant matter.

ORGANISM

An organism is an animal, a plant or a single-celled life form.

OXYGEN

Oxygen is a gas that makes up part of the air we breathe. It's highly reactive, which means it bonds easily with other elements (for example, carbon). Animals rely on oxygen to survive—they breathe it in and use it to convert nutrients into energy, releasing carbon dioxide as a waste product of this process. Plants exist in perfect symbiosis with animals, as they absorb carbon dioxide and release oxygen.

PARASITE

A parasite is an organism that makes its home in or on an organism of another species, relying on it for food, shelter, and everything else it needs to live. The organism that a parasite makes its home on is called its "host."

PIGMENT

Pigments are colored chemicals in the tissues of animals. Some animals produce their own pigments, whereas others get them from their food.

PLANKTON

Plankton are small living things—comprising both plants and animals—that drift along in the ocean and other bodies of water. Plankton is an essential food source for many animals, and certain types of plankton are also vital for releasing oxygen into the atmosphere.

POACHING

Animal poaching is the illegal capturing or killing of animals.

POLLUTION

Pollution is the introduction of harmful materials or substances into our environment. The three main types of pollution are water, air, and land pollution. Some examples of pollutants are microplastics in the ocean, greenhouse gas emissions in the atmosphere, and pesticides used in agriculture.

PREDATOR

In zoology, "predator" usually refers to an animal that hunts other animals for food. Parasites are also a kind of predator. Predators are essential to a balanced ecosystem.

SANCTUARY

A wildlife sanctuary is a carefully designed environment where endangered wild species are brought to live and be protected from human threats, such as poaching. Proper sanctuaries are as much like the animals' natural habitats as possible: they have the right climate, and contain the right variety of plant and animal species.

TERRESTRIAL

Terrestrial animals are those that spend all or most of their time on land.

TERRITORY

An animal's territory is the area of land or water that it lives in, claims as its own and defends against trespassers.

TIDE

The tide is the periodic rise and fall of the ocean. Changes in the tide are caused by the earth spinning around, and by the gravitational pull of the sun and the moon.

VERTEBRATE

Vertebrates are animals that have a spine and a well-developed skeleton inside their bodies.

WILD SPECIES

Wild species are animals that have evolved without human interference and live and reproduce independently from humans.

INDEX

ACKNOWLEDGMENTS

I'd like to thank Jane Novak for suggesting this project to me, and the fantastic team at Hardie Grant Egmont, especially Ella Meave. Without their dedication, this book would never have seen the light of day. I'd also like to thank Sam Caldwell for his brilliant illustrations, and Pooja Desai and Kristy Lund-White for their magnificent design work. I owe much gratitude to my wife Kate Holden and our son Coleby. They put up with long absences as I wrote this book. Many colleagues helped me with information, among whom Kris Helgen and Luigi Boitani deserve special mention.